DEAD MEN TALKING

D1438725

DEAD MEN TALKING

Nicholas Davies

MAINSTREAM
PUBLISHING
EDINBURGH AND LONDON

First published in Great Britain in 2004 by
MAINSTREAM PUBLISHING COMPANY (EDINBURGH) LTD
7 Albany Street
Edinburgh EH1 3UG

ISBN 1 84018 803 0

A catalogue record for this book
is available from the British Library

Typeset in Baskerville Book, Confidential
and Gill Sans Condensed

Printed and bound in Great Britain by
Mackays of Chatham plc

CONTENTS

GLOSSARY

14th Int. – 14th Intelligence Company

ASU – active service unit

E4A – the RUC's covert surveillance unit

EDO – Explosive Ordnance Disposal Officer

ETA – Euskadi Ta Askatasuna (Basque separatist terror group)

FRU – Force Research Unit

GCHQ – Government Communications Headquarters

HMSU – Headquarters Mobile Support Unit

INLA – Irish National Liberation Army

IRA – Irish Republican Army

KPPS – Key Person's Protection Scheme

MISR – Military Intelligence Source Reports

MRF – Mobile Reaction Forces

NCO – Non-commissioned Officer

NICRA – Northern Ireland Civil Rights Association

OIRA – Official IRA

PIRA – Provisional IRA

PLO – Palestine Liberation Organisation

PSNI – Police Service of Northern Ireland
QRF – Quick Reaction Force
RUC – Royal Ulster Constabulary
SAS – Special Air Service
SB – Special Branch
SDLP – Social Democratic and Labour Party
TCG – Tasking Coordination Group
UCBT – under-car booby-trap
UDA – Ulster Defence Association
UDR – Ulster Defence Regiment
UFF – Ulster Freedom Fighters
UPV – Ulster Protestant Volunteers
UVF – Ulster Volunteer Force
VCP – vehicle checkpoint

PREFACE

The three decades of Troubles that tore apart Northern Ireland and set Catholics against Protestants, Republicans against Loyalists, also caused major problems to successive British governments, their intelligence services and security services.

In *Dead Men Talking*, this author has traced and examined the governments' efforts to bring an end to the IRA's campaign of violence, both against mainland Britain and, in particular, against the Northern Ireland Protestants who bore the brunt of the Provisional IRA's determination to bring about a united Ireland. Desperate attempts were made by both Labour and Conservative administrations to stem the tide of murder, indiscriminate violence, bombings and shootings which wrecked lives and communities, making life almost unbearable for those caught up in the chaos and destruction of internecine warfare. This proved largely futile, however, until the Republicans at the heart of the Troubles became somewhat exhausted and decided instead to seek political solutions to some of their political demands.

This book reveals the tasks given to the intelligence and security services in what became a war against the 'Provos', and gives examples of the lengths, including murder, to which they were prepared to go to put an end to the IRA's violent campaigns.

Frequently, the intelligence services were prepared to 'fight fire with fire' and indulged in nefarious killings and shootings. In *Ten-Thirty-Three*, this author revealed the killings carried out with the assistance of British Military Intelligence. *Dead Men Talking* now reveals details of killings carried out with the assistance of the RUC Special Branch and MI5.

Also highlighted here is the most important and vital intelligence work carried out by various undercover agents in the Province, especially the extraordinary risks taken by Steak Knife, the British master spy at the very heart of the Provisional IRA. Without his help, many more innocent lives would have been lost and the Provos would have been far more successful in their bid to force a deal over the future of Northern Ireland through the use of bombs and terror.

I owe a deep debt of gratitude to three people who gave me great assistance, advice and information in writing this book: one who worked for British Military Intelligence, another who worked for many years with the RUC Special Branch and a third who spent a number of years in Northern Ireland working with MI5.

These three people agreed to help me so that the true facts of what really happened in Northern Ireland during the Troubles can be shared and better understood by those who lived in the Province through those desperate years.

Chapter One

A KILLING TOO FAR

On a cold, wet night in November 1988, mourners from an Orange Lodge met in Lisburn to pay their last respects to one of their Order who had died peacefully in his sleep after a long and successful life. As well as family members, there were also some dozen or so officers of the RUC's Special Branch (SB) present who had known the dead man, as well as some members of British Military Intelligence's elite Force Research Unit (FRU).

They were amongst friends, people they had grown up with and had come to trust. All were loyal and trusted members of the Order who understood full well that whatever was said on such occasions would not leave that gathering, for all members are sworn never to reveal secrets of the Lodge or the Order. And they rarely, if ever, do so. It is accepted among the fraternity that all conversations between members are treated with the same secrecy and confidence as the confessional.

At this particular gathering of men, with so many Special Branch officers present in their capacity as Lodge members, the conversation soon turned to the Troubles and the problems each of them faced in their daily lives. During the 30 years of internecine strife in the Province, and especially when the bombing campaigns of the Provisional IRA were at their height, many options these Special Branch officers were asked to weigh up and make a judgement upon had life-or-death consequences.

The word at this gathering was that something 'big' and 'highly controversial' was being mooted and it was expected that the Special Branch might well be tasked with carrying it out. Apparently the 'big' event was to be the killing of a single man which had been under discussion at the highest level for some two years.

In the parlance of those SB men, the 'highest level' meant only two things – senior politicians and MI5. The SB officers had also been led to understand that the killing, if carried out, would have repercussions throughout Northern Ireland and beyond, possibly even among politicians at the European Parliament.

The discussion left little doubt that plans were being drawn up for the murder of either a high-profile politician, a member of the Provisional IRA's Army Council or, possibly, a high-profile lawyer. This last prospect rang warning bells amongst those members of the FRU in attendance, as they were well aware that one of their agents, Brian Nelson, had been talking about planning the killing of Patrick Finucane, the Belfast solicitor who had spent many years fighting legal battles on behalf of Republicans and members of the Provisional IRA.

During the previous 12 months, Brian Nelson, who was working as an agent for the Force Research Unit while employed as the chief intelligence officer of the Loyalist Ulster Defence Association (UDA), had been urging his FRU handlers to provide him with detailed information about Finucane so that a UDA killer squad could assassinate him. Thanks, however, to a number of timely interventions by FRU handlers and senior officers, attempts on Finucane's life had been successfully thwarted. Those FRU handlers had taken steps to ensure Finucane's safety on at least four separate occasions when plans for his murder had been organised, the killer squad put on stand-by and the briefing for the operation had taken place.

The days following the 1988 Lisburn funeral became weeks, and nothing earth shattering occurred. Bombs were occasionally set off by the Provos, people were sometimes shot and killed on both sides of the political divide, and families tended to stay in their homes at night rather than risk going out to the town and city centres. The tense, nervous, some would say hellish, existence that citizens of Northern Ireland had lived through during the previous decade continued much as before.

During this time, the FRU handlers, waiting impatiently for the expected dramatic event, noted that Brian Nelson had become unusually quiet and had stopped pestering them to give the green light for the UDA to kill Patrick Finucane. Nelson's handlers still believed that something was being planned, however, and wondered if the big event had simply been postponed after more sober heads had prevailed, or whether Finucane was not the main target as they had initially suspected.

At 2 p.m. on the afternoon of Sunday, 12 February 1989, the RUC set up roadblocks within a few hundred yards of the Finucane home. There was nothing unusual or dramatic about that event, for police roadblocks were constantly being set up all over Belfast, in both Republican and Loyalist areas, for a myriad of different reasons. On this occasion, the roadblock had been set up at the express request of the RUC Special Branch, and, in the usual way, the Tasking Coordination Group (TCG) – comprising senior officers from MI5, the RUC Special Branch and British Military Intelligence – was informed. Informing the TCG of the roadblock meant that all other security services would be warned to keep away from that area because a security operation was being carried out. That operation could simply be a random check of vehicles entering and leaving the area or, of course, it could be something more sinister. At five o'clock, the roadblocks were dismantled and taken away, the RUC officers returned to their bases and quiet settled once again on the residential area. The area was now clean, clear of security services, permitting easy access for the murder squad.

Just before 7.30 p.m., a taxi came to a halt a short distance from the home of Patrick Finucane. Two men got out of the taxi, one carrying a hold-all. The driver waited in the car. As they walked along the road, they checked to see if anyone was about. All was quiet. They walked into the front garden of the Finucane home and the man carrying the hold-all put it down near the front door, taking out two weapons and two balaclavas. Each man quickly pulled a balaclava over his head, checked once again to see no one was around and one of them knocked on the front door. His accomplice stood back out of sight. The first man then tested the door handle and, much to his surprise, the door opened. As he took a step inside, Patrick Finucane opened the kitchen door, and the two men stood opposite each other just ten feet apart.

Patrick Finucane, his wife Geraldine and their three children had just sat down in their kitchen for their evening meal when the knock came at the front door. Patrick got to his feet to see who was there but before he had time to leave the kitchen he was confronted by a masked man pointing a handgun at him. Without giving him a chance to react, the gunman fired twice, hitting Finucane in the chest. He fell to the floor. Finucane's wife Geraldine and their three children froze in horror. Then the other masked man, carrying a sub-machine gun, came into the kitchen shouting to everyone, 'Keep quiet; don't move!'

He moved closer to Patrick Finucane's prone body, pointed the weapon at his chest and pulled the trigger. The gunman continued firing for some four seconds as he stood over Finucane, riddling his body with bullets. It was at that moment that Geraldine and the three children found their voices and screamed at the men and the horror that was unfolding before them. One bullet hit Mrs Finucane in the leg but none of the three children was injured in the attack. In all, 14 rounds were fired at Finucane.

The gunmen then turned and ran out of the house to the waiting taxi, ripping off their balaclavas as they ran. The vehicle, which had been hijacked earlier that evening, was later found abandoned at the junction of the Loyalist Forthriver and Ballygomartin roads. Geraldine Finucane ran to the phone, called the emergency services and then turned to comfort her distraught and frightened children. Patrick Finucane's body was lifeless and Geraldine knew instinctively that her husband was dead. Some ten minutes elapsed before the RUC and an ambulance arrived.

Almost immediately after the RUC began their investigation, detectives said that the killing bore all the hallmarks of a Loyalist paramilitary group. The following day, the UFF, a cover name assumed by the UDA's killing squad, claimed responsibility for the murder. But who really wanted Patrick Finucane dead, and why?

Immediately after receiving the news of the murder, Tom King, the Secretary of State for Northern Ireland, expressed his horror at the killing:

> No civilised society can tolerate murder from whichever vicious extreme it comes. The deaths of every one of the seven people murdered so far this year – some by the IRA, some by Loyalist extremists – show the total futility and awfulness of killing. The police and security services will do all they can to bring the perpetrators to justice. Everyone in Northern Ireland must help in ending this awful cycle of violence.

Three weeks prior to the killing, however, a junior Home Office Minister, Douglas Hogg, had made an inflammatory speech in the House of Commons in which he suggested that certain Northern Irish solicitors were 'unduly sympathetic' to terrorists. Hogg's statement caused a storm of protest in the Province's legal circles and amongst Unionist politicians as well as those representing Republican interests, but Home Office spokesmen made it plain that the Minister stood by his controversial comments.

On the day following the Finucane killing, the President of the Law Society of Northern Ireland, Colin Haddick, accused Hogg of having created an 'excuse' for terrorists to carry out murders.

> We are on record at the time Mr Hogg made the statement as having expressed our disbelief at what he said. If Mr Hogg had specific cause for concern about solicitors generally or as individuals, there are well-known channels through which he could have had such matters investigated. Let me add that the Law Society has never once been asked to investigate the conduct of any solicitor. What Mr Hogg has done is to create an excuse for terrorist organisations to carry out murders – something which was not available to them before.

What Mr Haddick was not aware of was that Mr Hogg's extraordinary speech, which appeared to have come out of the blue, had been planned well in advance. In fact, it had been drafted by senior MI5 officers and Mr Hogg had been specifically requested to make the statement at that time, January 1989. The decision to murder Patrick Finucane had been taken some time in early January by those ultimately responsible for organising his death, who it can now be revealed were senior MI5 officers in London. Those MI5 officers were therefore well satisfied by the statement issued by Colin Haddick after Finucane's death, for it was precisely the reaction they had hoped for. Their goal to be rid of the lawyer had finally been achieved and, thanks to Mr Haddick's remarks, MI5 officers were confident that those actually behind the murder would never be traced and brought to justice.

Other revelations that helped direct the spotlight away from MI5 were allegations that for some months before Finucane's murder a number of RUC officers had been deliberately fostering a sense of frustration and anger amongst Loyalists about the lawyers defending Republicans and Catholics. Indeed, Amnesty International in London recorded allegations against a number of RUC officers engaged in such negative verbal attacks. These accusations were also taken up and given wider publicity by the Lawyers Committee for Human Rights. Included in the allegations was a claim by UDA members detained at Castlereagh prior to Finucane's murder that Special Branch officers had told them on numerous occasions that Patrick Finucane and other lawyers were doing everything in their power to keep Provo gunmen out of prison and on the streets of Belfast. Within days of the shooting, UDA sources made the claim to detectives and FRU officers that the RUC had in effect encouraged them to target Finucane.

It was not, of course, the first time that the RUC and, in particular, the RUC Special Branch, had been accused of involvement in killings in the Province. Unsurprisingly, the RUC's most frequent accusers were the Provisional IRA and other Republican supporters. Most of the allegations against the RUC had resulted from the deaths of men suspected of being members of the Provisional IRA, or known Republican activists; never before had they been accused of killing a well-known member of the legal establishment. The finger of suspicion was already pointing away from the men responsible for Finucane's murder. It was precisely the outcome MI5 had hoped and planned for.

Patrick Finucane was 38 at the time of his murder. He had spent the best part of his working life fighting for the rights of disadvantaged Catholics and Republicans, and he frequently represented those who had been arrested and charged with crimes including murder and offences against the Prevention of Terrorism Act. Finucane had studied his craft well and fought doggedly for his clients on every occasion, as any good solicitor should. As a result, his profile had risen significantly throughout the 1980s as he defended more and more Republicans, some of whom were members of the Provisional IRA, for example the IRA hunger strikers Bobby Sands and Pat McGeown.

It was in the early 1980s that suspicions were first raised that the young Finucane was rather too close to the Republican movement. His increasingly high-profile involvement caught the attention of MI5, the government department responsible for planning and coordinating intelligence work throughout Northern Ireland, and senior security service officers came to the conclusion that Finucane was not simply a Catholic lawyer acting for the Republicans of Northern Ireland whenever they had need of legal advice but something more sinister. He was placed under discreet, long-distance surveillance, and intelligence about his contacts, his clients and his close ties with Republicanism was noted, logged and added to his burgeoning file. One of Finucane's brothers, John, had been killed while on active service with the IRA and another brother had been engaged to Mairead Farrell, one of the IRA volunteers shot dead by the SAS in Gibraltar. When claiming responsibility for his death, the UFF had said that they killed 'Pat Finucane the Provisional IRA officer, not Pat Finucane the solicitor', but police investigating the murder said there was no evidence to support the claim that he had been a member of the IRA.

As a result of close surveillance, MI5 had discovered that Patrick Finucane had become close, indeed very close, to Gerry Adams, a person whom the security services had identified as one of the most intelligent and ruthless of the Provo leaders. Finucane and Adams had been working together, spending hours talking to each other, discussing Sinn Fein, the Provos, the political and security situation in Northern Ireland, as well as care for the families of jailed Republicans. The talks had begun in earnest after Adams had been promoted to become Provo Commander of the IRA's Belfast Brigade in the late 1970s, when he took over responsibility for briefing and giving orders to Provo active service units (ASUs) which were responsible for conducting bombing campaigns against the British Army, the RUC, prison officers and Loyalists as part of the Provisional IRA's bid to create a single, unified Ireland. In the process of their murderous campaign, of course, the Provos killed many innocent men, women and children, more often than not blown to pieces by an indiscriminate bomb. And these bombers were the people the forces of law and order were engaged in fighting and, if possible, arresting and bringing to justice.

At the same time, MI6, Britain's overseas secret intelligence agency which was responsible for keeping a watchful eye on Republicanism in the Irish Republic, was also tasked with gathering any intelligence concerning Finucane and on-passing that information to MI5.

Finucane drew further attention to himself during his struggle to end the Diplock Court system in the Province. These anti-terrorist courts differed substantially from ordinary courts of justice as only one judge presided and there was no jury. The strategy was an attempt to contain the terrorists as far as possible by means of legal procedures, instead of military force and extra-judicial measures such as detention without trial, both of which fed the Provos' propaganda that they were fighting a war of liberation against a foreign enemy on their own soil. The Diplock Courts were ferociously opposed not only by Sinn Fein but also by many lawyers, human-rights groups and liberal-minded MPs in the House of Commons.

The Diplock Courts provided protection for witnesses. All witnesses, including RUC and Special Branch officers, could give their evidence without being identified in open court. This increased the confidence of many potential witnesses who were fearful of giving evidence in case they or their families became targets for Provo gunmen.

The other reason given for the introduction of Diplock Courts was that in ordinary jury trials of IRA terrorists, problems had arisen when other members of the Provisional IRA would try to discover the names and addresses of the 12 men and women sitting on each jury and put pressure on them to throw out the case against the defendants. Indeed, some jury members were threatened that if they didn't vote to clear the defendant, they and their families might be at risk. Though the names and addresses of jury members were never given out and every endeavour was made to conceal their identities, their personal details did on some occasions somehow still get into the hands of the Provos.

MI5 would later allege that they had learned that one of the people responsible for providing the names and addresses of witnesses to the Provisional IRA was Patrick Finucane. Other lawyers who defended Provo members were also put under suspicion but the person believed to be the central figure in revealing the details of witnesses was Finucane. No evidence was ever provided to substantiate this claim, however, and it was fiercely denied by his family and colleagues.

Finucane fought hard to put an end to the Diplock Courts because, he argued, they denied the defendant the basic right to be tried by a jury. Of course, as a lawyer who believed in the justice system, he was right to do so. Juries are an essential part of any civilised trial in a democracy and, of course, all lawyers should defend that principle, as Finucane did. His appeals to higher legal authorities in the UK fell on deaf ears, however, so Finucane decided to take his legal argument to the European Court of Justice in The Hague. He hoped to persuade the European judges to declare the Diplock Courts 'illegal' and 'unconstitutional', but he failed.

Understandably, Patrick Finucane's attempt to put an end to the Diplock Courts annoyed the British Government and angered senior officers in all sections of the security services, particularly the RUC, who, understandably, had welcomed them for the protection they gave officers and their families. Court records also revealed that the Diplock Courts returned more guilty verdicts against terrorists than had been the case when juries sat in judgement.

The rebuttal from Europe, however, only convinced Patrick Finucane that there was a cause to be fought and he continued defending many Republicans and Provo suspects in the Diplock Courts. The more cases Finucane fought, it seemed, the more chance the defendants had of getting off the charges brought against them. Indeed, Patrick Finucane became something of a hero in the Republican clubs of west Belfast, though he didn't see himself in that vein. He believed he was simply involved in seeing that justice was being carried out in Northern Ireland and that defendants were treated fairly.

Finucane's high profile and close connections to the Republican movement, notably the professional advice he was giving to Gerry Adams and other senior Provos, effectively sealed his fate. And he then played into the hands of MI5 by his close involvement in what became known as the 'shoot-to-kill' cases, when he acted for the widow of Gervaise McKerr at a long-running inquest into the circumstances surrounding his death and also represented Martin McCauley, who was injured in one of the attacks.

Gervaise McKerr was gunned down in cold blood along with two of his friends by an RUC Headquarters Mobile Support Unit (HMSU) after a high-speed car chase near Lurgan. His death was the first of six in the final weeks of 1982 which led to accusations that the RUC was practising a policy of 'shoot-to-kill' in Northern Ireland. The second incident occurred on 24 November 1982 and resulted in the death of 17-year-old Michael Tighe and serious injury to his friend, 19-year-old Martin McCauley; the third, in which Seamus Grew and Roderick Carroll were shot, took place on 12 December.

Though the manner of McKerr's death is well documented, it is worth noting the horrendous details which rocketed this particular killing to such prominence. The sequence of events leading to McKerr's death, and those of others with whom he was associated at the time, is crucial to those Republicans and others who remain convinced that some RUC officers had been given the go-ahead to take lethal measures against suspected terrorists by senior staff in the RUC and MI5.

On 27 October 1982, an anonymous phone call, supposedly from a member of the public, was received at Lurgan police station informing officers that a motorcycle had been found abandoned on a dirt track called the Kinnego embankment. Three uniformed RUC officers, Sergeant Sean Quinn and Constables Paul Hamilton and Alan McCloy, were sent to check it out. Ten minutes later, an explosion rocked the area and the three officers were blown to pieces. Explosives experts discovered that the bombers had planted a booby-trap bomb in a culvert beneath the embankment which had exploded when the officers walked over it. To the horror and extreme embarrassment of the security forces, forensic experts found that the explosives used to kill the three officers were part of a 1,000 lb shipment which plain-clothes officers of E4A, the RUC's covert surveillance unit, had previously watched being unloaded and stored in a local hay barn after a tip-off from MI5.

These explosives had been hidden in what was known as Kitty's Barn, close to a staunchly Republican housing estate on the outskirts of Lurgan. Officers from MI5, trained in counter-terrorist operations, installed highly sophisticated listening devices in the roof of the barn. These were specifically programmed to pick up not only conversations inside the barn but also any other noises suggesting the explosives or arms were being moved.

To ensure the total security of the explosives, a standing observation post was set up, to be manned 24 hours a day by the Det – so-called because soldiers from the SAS were 'detached' from their regiment to serve in Ulster for two-year stints. This unit was detailed to stay out of sight but keep a watching eye on the barn. The security services, backed by the RUC, hoped to track whoever moved the explosives, discover the Provos' target and capture the bombers red-handed. From sources inside the IRA, the Tasking Coordination Group had learned that the explosives had been brought in to launch a specific attack on the security forces, but they had no idea where or when this attack would take place. Importantly, the security services also had no clue as to the identity of the Provo active service unit that had been ordered to carry out the attack.

Unbelievably, however, no one at MI5, the Det or the TCG had deemed it necessary to inform Lurgan RUC of exactly what was going on at Kitty's Barn and the three officers were allowed to walk straight into the terrorists' trap. The MI5 listening device and the Det surveillance operation also proved to be a total failure. First, the Det patrol detailed to watch the barn had been taken off duty for a 24-hour break, but no one had been informed of that decision. Second, the highly sophisticated listening device installed in the barn by MI5 was so delicate and high-tech that wind and rain had rendered it useless. After the tragic deaths of the three officers, another tried-and-tested listening device was fitted to the handle of the barn door, where, MI5 technicians insisted, it would not be affected by adverse weather conditions. The Det were also ordered to keep a permanent 24-hour watch on the barn and not to move without permission from the TCG.

The deaths of the three RUC officers raised a storm of questions and recriminations inside MI5, the security services, the Det and the RUC. There had been an appalling lack of communication between the various strands of the security services, and, as a result, three officers had been killed. No senior officer at Lurgan RUC station even thought it necessary to inform either the HMSU or the TCG of the cold-blooded killing of the three officers, showing that there were defects up and down the line of communication.

A few weeks later, E4A learned from informants inside the IRA that two of the main suspects believed to be responsible for planting the Kinnego culvert booby-trap bomb – Sean Burns and Eugene Toman, who were both 21 – had returned to the Province after fleeing south of the border following the deaths of the three officers.

On 11 November, officers from E4A discovered that Burns and Toman were staying at the home of Gervaise McKerr, who lived in Avondale Green, near Lurgan. Within minutes of this piece of intelligence being received by the TCG, an HMSU team was dispatched to the area. Wearing the traditional dark-green uniforms of the RUC, driving an unmarked police car and heavily armed, the three members of the HMSU team had only just arrived in Lurgan when E4A radioed that Burns and Toman had left the house and were being driven away by McKerr. It was shortly after 8 p.m. and the night sky was cloudy and dark.

The HMSU patrol checked their weapons and set up an impromptu vehicle checkpoint near a T-junction. As the car approached the junction, the HMSU vehicle parked on the left side was blocking half of the narrow road, with one armed officer on the right side waving a red light, warning the approaching car to stop. The Provo car slowed almost to a halt and then accelerated hard, forcing the officer to leap out of the way. He did, however, manage to fire off five shots from his Ruger mini-14 rifle, shattering the car's rear window and hitting the man in the back seat. He also managed to puncture one of the rear tyres.

As the Provo car raced away, swerving wildly across the road, the HMSU officers jumped in their car and took off in pursuit. While racing after the Provo car, two of the HMSU team grabbed their Sterling machine guns and opened fire, Chicago gangster-style, leaning out of the windows and firing at the getaway car. When the speeding Provos' car came to a roundabout, driving at some 70 mph, the driver tried to turn right, lost control and careered off the road and down an embankment.

The three officers screeched to a halt, leapt out of their vehicle, ran to the edge of the embankment and began firing at the Provos' car below. They poured a total of 117 rounds into the getaway car. When the firing stopped, the officers carefully approached the vehicle to discover the bodies of the three men shot to pieces. So devastating was the firepower used that the young men were virtually unrecognisable. Police called in to investigate and report on the deaths found no weapons in the car.

The killing of three unarmed young men – McKerr, Toman and Burns – caused a furore and quickly became a cause célèbre for the political wing of Sinn Fein. Here was proof, they claimed, if proof was needed, that the RUC were carrying out a shoot-to-kill policy. In a shattered car outside the town of Lurgan in Northern Ireland, three unarmed young men had been killed while fleeing from a pursuing unmarked police car, cut to ribbons by armed officers. Their deaths became one of Sinn Fein's golden pieces of evidence with which to win thousands of Irish-Americans to their cause and bring tens of thousands of US dollars into the Sinn Fein coffers as the Irish-American clubs urged their members to support the armed struggle against the occupying British Army. It was magnificent propaganda and, of course, Sinn Fein milked it to the last drop. Indeed, it would take some 20 years until the money from Irish-American sources began to dry up.

Throughout both the north and south of Ireland, Sinn Fein claimed the shooting had been a 'summary execution'. The respective families of the young men denied that any of them was a member of the Provisional IRA and claimed that, had the police wanted, all three could have been arrested at home at any time. However, the men were given paramilitary-style funerals and the North Armagh Brigade of the IRA claimed that all three were members of their organisation. Black berets, gloves and Irish tricolours were placed on their coffins, and at the graveside a single shot was fired over the coffins by a masked man.

But that was not the end of the matter. To appease world opinion as much as anything, the British Government permitted the Director of Public Prosecutions to charge the three police officers involved – Montgomery, Brannigan and Robinson – with the murder of Eugene Toman. Understandably, this move infuriated the RUC, the security services and the British Army, and was a severe blow to morale for all those engaged in fighting the

Provisional IRA. Indeed, many felt the prosecution was a betrayal of colleagues who risked their lives on a daily basis in the never-ending battle against terrorism.

In June 1984, the three officers were acquitted of Toman's murder and the judge, Lord Justice Maurice Gibson, appeared to reveal that the prosecutions had been ordered on political grounds when he stated:

> The prosecution's failure at the preliminary inquiry to disclose information at its disposal . . . had left the presiding magistrate . . . with a very partial picture, and I do not think I am putting this too far if I say a false picture, of the circumstances of the shooting.

Lord Gibson, however, added fuel to the fire of accusations that there was an official shoot-to-kill policy by praising the acquitted officers for bringing the deceased men to 'the final court of justice'. The judge and his wife were later murdered by the IRA.

It was in 1984, five years before Finucane's murder, that John Stalker, then the Deputy Chief Constable of the Greater Manchester Police Force, was asked to undertake an inquiry into the deaths of the six men who had been killed in late 1982 by members of the RUC. As Stalker pursued his investigation in the Province, he became increasingly alarmed by the resistance and obstruction he encountered from RUC officers at all levels. He became convinced that he was getting near the truth about some of the deaths when, at the very moment he was about to gain access to evidence which could have seriously embarrassed the RUC, he was dramatically relieved of his duties.

Four years later, John Stalker wrote a calm, honest book, *The Stalker Affair*, an account of his investigation and the conclusions he was able to draw. He did not claim in his book that he knew with 'absolute certainty' the truth of what he uncovered. However, he did conclude that in a five-week period in the midwinter of 1982, six men were shot dead by a specialist squad of police officers and the circumstances pointed to a police inclination, if not a policy, to shoot suspects dead without warning rather than to arrest them. He wrote, 'Coming, as these incidents did, so close together, the suspicion of deliberate assassination was not unreasonable.'

In September 1985, Stalker submitted a massive and detailed report in 16 book-form volumes, some 3,600 pages long, to the RUC Chief Constable Sir John Hermon, recommending the prosecutions of 11 police officers, ranging in rank from police constables to Chief Superintendent, for a variety of criminal offences, including conspiracy to pervert the course of justice and perjury. It also linked the six 'shoot-to-kill' deaths to the earlier deaths of the three police officers and contained dozens of recommendations for changes in policy, as well as criticism of many areas of policing including, specifically, the way the three investigations had been handled.

Stalker wrote:

> It was well known to the Home Office and other government officials, including MI5 officers, that my renewed enquiries would, by law, have involved discussions with the Northern Ireland Police Authority if at any stage I suspected disciplinary offences on the part of senior officers.

The paths of John Stalker and Patrick Finucane crossed when Stalker began investigations into a case in which Finucane had represented Martin McCauley, the friend of Michael Tighe who had somehow managed to survive the RUC shooting in Kitty's Barn in November 1982. McCauley was being prosecuted for possessing three old rifles that had been found in the barn after the shooting. While pursuing his investigation, Stalker needed to interview Finucane at length to see if he could throw some light on the matter. Later, Stalker wrote in his book:

> A youngish RUC uniformed sergeant . . . left his group and
> approached me angrily after a very short conversation with
> a solicitor representing Martin McCauley, the youth who
> had survived the shooting at the Hayshed. [He] said: 'The
> solicitor [Finucane] is an IRA man – any man who
> represents IRA men is worse than an IRA man. His brother
> is an IRA man also and I have to say that I believe a senior
> policeman of your rank should not be seen speaking to the
> likes of either of them. My colleagues have asked me to tell
> you that you have embarrassed all of us in doing that.'

Such a remark from a uniformed sergeant may have alerted Stalker
to the probability that he was getting near the truth: that there was
indeed some form of collusion in the killings by the RUC. But
Stalker realised full well that one off-the-record conversation with
one officer would prove nothing. He needed to keep digging.

One of the crucial areas of Stalker's investigation concerned a
tape recording of a conversation that had taken place inside the
staked-out hayshed, Kitty's Barn, on the night when Tighe was
shot dead and McCauley wounded by members of a special RUC
anti-terrorist unit. The local community had been outraged by the
shootings because Tighe had no criminal record and had never
been involved in political or terrorist activity. McCauley, however,
had some rather tenuous connections with suspected terrorists.

Unbeknown to the officers involved in the shooting and those
present at McCauley's trial, including Lord Justice Kelly, the events
of that fateful day had been recorded by a second electronic
listening device that had been additionally sited in the barn after
the deaths of the three police officers a few weeks earlier. Although
the explosives and arms had been moved from the barn, it
obviously still remained of great interest to the security services.

The tape revealed that McCauley and Tighe had walked into a
sophisticated operation that had been camouflaged to look like a
chance encounter. The battle over that tape dominated the legal

arguments between the Crown lawyers and the defence team before, during and after the trial, though, for legal reasons, it could not be introduced in open court during the trial. The repercussions over the tape came to affect the political agenda in Northern Ireland and London, the highest echelons of both the security and intelligence services and the British Government's approach to the future policing of the Province. It became the focus of a bitter struggle between those who believed that the tape could provide evidence of unlawful killing by police officers and those who remain convinced that details of intelligence gathering should remain classified.

After much wrangling, the most senior MI5 officers in London eventually gave Stalker full authority to hear the tape, but Sir John Hermon, then Chief Constable of the RUC, declined to hand it over, hinting that the tape 'may not exist'. Eventually, however, Sir John Hermon told Stalker that he would be given the tape.

But nothing happened. No tape was handed over. No one even contacted Stalker and no one in MI5 or Sir John Hermon's office returned his phone calls.

Months later, MI5 once again agreed to hand over the tape to Stalker but at a meeting with Sir John Hermon shortly afterwards, the Chief Constable told him, 'You can never have the tape, I am afraid. The tape has been destroyed but a transcript exists.'

Sir John then told Stalker that both he and his team members could only read the tape transcripts after signing a form designed and used by the Special Branch as a declaration of secrecy. To his great credit, Stalker refused, knowing full well that this was a blatant attempt to confuse and obstruct the search for evidence in Northern Ireland.

It can now be revealed that, in fact, the entire episode of the secret tape had been an elaborate charade played out by MI5, which appeared to be supporting John Stalker and his inquiry, while the Chief Constable of the RUC appeared to be the only person refusing to assist Stalker in his investigation by refusing to hand over the tape for scrutiny. In reality, of course, that was not the case at all. MI5 and their political masters in London knew that if that tape had been heard in open court, there was every probability that the RUC anti-terrorist squad who killed Tighe would have had to face charges of murder. It was simply a step too far for MI5 and the British Government to take, as it would have had a devastating effect on the morale of the RUC, the army and the Protestants of Northern Ireland, who would then have felt they were having to fight the Provos with one hand tied behind their backs.

After submitting his first report to the Chief Constable of the RUC in September 1985, Stalker never returned to Northern Ireland. He was permanently removed from the investigation. Two years later, Stalker, then aged only 47, was all but forced to leave the police force despite the fact he should have had at least eight more years to serve. He had done his task too well. He had investigated too thoroughly and he had come within an ace of discovering that some killings of members and supporters of the Provisional IRA had not been carried out by rogue elements within the RUC but had been authorised by senior RUC Special Branch officers. This author has been unable to ascertain whether Stalker actually did discover if any such killings had been authorised, condoned or encouraged by MI5 officers in Northern Ireland.

In July 1986, Tom King, the Secretary of State for Northern Ireland, revealed that Sir John Hermon had statutorily approved Stalker's removal from the inquiry into the RUC after consultation with the Attorney General. The inquiry had come to a shameful end, but that had been inevitable from the moment John Stalker set out to investigate honestly certain killings, all of which had been closely monitored by, and, nearly always, carried out with the full knowledge of, senior officers in both the Special Branch and MI5.

The shoot-to-kill incidents were therefore obviously an issue of extreme controversy at this particularly dark stage of the Troubles, and it was into this morass that Patrick Finucane waded when he agreed to represent the family of Gervaise McKerr at the long-running inquest into his death. Five different coroners were appointed to handle the proceedings at different stages and one of the main points of contention was whether or not the RUC officers involved in the shootings would be required to give evidence. Finucane was insistent that the officers appear at the hearings to justify their actions in the shooting of McKerr, Burns and Toman. This demand was refused at first, but Finucane finally won a High Court action forcing the officers to give evidence. The Government, however, challenged the decision in the House of Lords and won in March 1990. By that time Patrick Finucane was dead.

The young firebrand lawyer had come to be seen as a thorn in the side of the Establishment, the British Government, senior MI5 officers and the Protestant Loyalists, many of whom had come to believe that the entire Catholic minority were guilty of all terrorist crimes unless proved innocent. MI5 had come to the conclusion that Finucane was more than just an able young lawyer fighting for justice; he had become involved in the Republican movement and their fight for a united Ireland. He was getting in the way of their plans and this would not be tolerated for long.

It was some five years after John Stalker had been 'informed' that Pat Finucane was an IRA suspect that another senior police officer from England, John Stevens, then the Chief Constable of Cambridgeshire, was asked to head an investigation into charges of possible collusion between the security forces and the Protestant paramilitaries in Northern Ireland. It was suspected by some that the security forces were providing information and documents containing the details of possible targets to Loyalist terrorists. The tall, jovial 'copper's copper' thought the whole inquiry would be over in a matter of weeks.

Some 13 years later, a senior colleague of John Stevens would say:

> We thought it was going to be a fairly routine investigation. We didn't expect to find that there was much to the allegations of collusion, quite honestly. The claim that officers from the security forces had supplied Loyalist gunmen with the names and addresses of people they thought were terrorists in order to have them murdered seemed too fantastic to have any basis.

The inquiry would eventually discover that, far from being fantastic, the allegation was true. The truth of that collusion was first revealed in *Ten-Thirty-Three*, published in 1997, which told of Brian Nelson, the UDA's chief intelligence officer who was also working for the British Army's secret Force Research Unit.

The events leading up to Patrick Finucane's killing would eventually be closely traced by the team of detectives under Sir John Stevens. They discovered that 18 months before Finucane's murder, Brian Nelson approached his handler in the Force Research Unit to request details on Finucane so that the UDA could plan his murder.

At the meeting in September 1987, Nelson told his handlers that Finucane had been singled out as he seemed to be acting as a mouthpiece for the Provos and this made him a fair target. His handlers pointed out that Finucane was a very well-known figure and that Nelson did not need their help to identify him, but he pressed them to provide him with details of the lawyer's everyday movements so the UDA could carefully plan their attack.

When his handlers refused to help him, Nelson left in high dudgeon. Before leaving, he was told in strong terms that if the UDA were planning to target Finucane then he must inform his handlers. But his handlers had little faith that Nelson would do so.

Nelson was quiet for a few months and then came back to tell his FRU handlers that a decision had been taken at the very top of the UDA to kill Finucane. The plan was to shoot the solicitor as he was driving away from the Crumlin Road courthouse and Nelson told the handlers that he had already carried out a recce:

> When Finucane leaves Court at the end of the day, he drives along Crumlin Road for a few hundred yards before turning left and heads along a side road towards north Belfast. That leads to a Protestant area. Along that road he has to slow down and it's there we plan to ambush him. It'll be a piece of cake. He never has any bodyguards and we have examined his car and found that it isn't even armoured, so there should be no problem.

Nelson also told them that no specific date had been fixed for the shooting but added, 'It'll be very soon, we're ready to go.'

Within minutes of that meeting ending, senior FRU officers were informed and the facts reported 'as a matter of urgency' to the TCG, which came to the same conclusion as the FRU – that everything possible must be done to stop the UDA killing Finucane. Orders were immediately issued to the army and the RUC to swamp the Crumlin Road Court area and a square mile around it for as long as the current case was being heard. The officers were not told why they had to do this nor whose life they were there to protect. More importantly, the decision was also taken at TCG level not to inform Patrick Finucane that he had been targeted by the UDA gunmen, a decision that has been much criticised by the lawyer's family. It was, however, common practice *not* to inform people who had been targeted because they would then have been entitled to demand police protection. So many people were allegedly targeted by the terrorists that it would have been impossible for the RUC to protect them all. Instead, after evaluating all the circumstances, the RUC, often with the help of the army and the security services, found ways to prevent any action being taken – as in this case, by swamping the area with extra forces, for example, until it was judged the danger had passed. There were literally hundreds of occasions when this policy was satisfactorily pursued.

To further ensure Finucane's safety, senior officers of E4A and the Det surveillance units were summoned to an urgent meeting and told of the UDA plot to assassinate Finucane. Both E4A and Det units were drafted into the area and ordered to keep a close eye on Finucane as he went about his everyday affairs. As each day passed and no overt attempt was made, the senior officers began to relax.

But Nelson knew the FRU had betrayed his confidence and flooded the area with army and police following his tip-off. He was furious, yelling at his handlers and accusing them of putting him in danger. After much shouting and swearing, Nelson quietened down and his FRU handlers again told him that he must persuade his UDA masters not to target Finucane because he was a solicitor and a member of the Establishment. 'There are limits to our work and your work,' he was told, 'and don't you ever forget that.'

Independently, however, as has previously been established, senior MI5 officers in the Province had already ordered round-the-clock surveillance on Finucane by their own officers on the ground. They had discovered that Finucane frequently held after-hours meetings away from his own Belfast offices with senior Sinn Fein/IRA activists. With sophisticated listening devices, MI5 had discovered that Finucane and those representing Sinn Fein/IRA discussed a range of topics which were not strictly legal matters. Crucially, however, there was never any proof that Finucane was involved in discussing possible targets to be attacked or in any way condoning attacks by Provo gunmen, bombers or active service units.

In March 1988, Nelson told his FRU handlers that Finucane was once again their number-one target and this time the UDA were determined to get him. Nelson told them that the UDA were convinced that Finucane was a Provo, working with Sinn Fein/IRA. When asked how he could be so sure, he informed them that they had been keeping a close watch on the solicitor's activities and were also disgusted by his success rate in securing the freedom of Republican suspects.

Nelson initially refused to give details of the plan, but, eventually, after much persuasion, he agreed, warning his handlers not to interfere this time as it would put him at serious risk.

The new plan was another ambush, similar to the last one, except that on this occasion Finucane would be attacked shortly after he had left his Belfast office at the end of a day's work. Using a gunman riding pillion on the back of a motorbike, they planned to hit the lawyer during his journey home.

Once again the TCG was informed of the plot to kill Finucane and once again the UDA plan was thwarted when the area around his Belfast office was covered each day with RUC officers and army patrols, making any attempt to get near the Belfast solicitor an impossibility. An angry Brian Nelson returned to FRU headquarters furious that the UDA plan had again been physically obstructed.

During the summer of 1988, Brian Nelson reported to the FRU on two further separate occasions that attempts were to be made by the UDA to kill Finucane, but each time the attempts came to nought as the Force Research Unit gave full details of the forthcoming attacks to the TCG. To the FRU handlers it seemed extraordinary that Nelson would keep returning to them to seek their approval for an attack on Finucane when they had thwarted each and every planned attack during the previous 12 months. They began to suspect there was some other hidden hand behind these plots: that some other intelligence organisation wanted FRU to sanction the attack and give the go-ahead so that at any future time British Military Intelligence would take the rap and be held responsible for organising the murder of Patrick Finucane. FRU handlers and officers knew that there were really only two possibilities – the RUC Special Branch or MI5.

Those serving on the TCG had been kept fully informed by the

FRU of the UDA's plans to kill Finucane and had taken active steps to prevent any attack. However, there had been no warning of any other planned attacks from either MI5 or the RUC Special Branch, and the Special Branch in particular had very close relations with the UDA. Special Branch officers had first infiltrated the ranks of the UDA in the late 1970s but many SB officers also drank with UDA Loyalists, had friends and relatives in their ranks and were often members of the same Lodge, the same football team. As one Loyalist put it, 'Every time the UDA moves a muscle the SB are aware.'

Of course, Sir John Stevens and his senior officers knew that there was a close relationship between the UDA and the Special Branch but they were not unduly concerned about that relationship until the night of 10 January 1990, when the room in the inquiry headquarters where the Stevens team stored their files, documents and records mysteriously caught fire. Every single document in the room was destroyed. And yet this room, electronically protected, was at the heart of what was supposed to be the RUC's most heavily guarded and secure building in Northern Ireland. That mystery fire changed the thinking of Sir John and his senior officers. Now there was deep suspicion of the RUC Special Branch. Later, the Stevens team would discover that, moments before the fire started, both the fire and intruder alarms had been turned off, but, unsurprisingly, they could find no one who would admit to having turned off those alarms. Those facts transformed the inquiry team's view of the entire situation in Northern Ireland. Collusion was now at the centre of their investigation. It has remained so ever since.

And yet, somewhat surprisingly, the team's first report, published in May 1990, after eight months of research, was cautious in the line it took. The report concluded that any collusion between the security forces and the paramilitaries had been 'neither widespread nor institutionalised' and had involved only the ad hoc leaking to Loyalists of standard security force documents –

documents available in any police station. In the light of subsequent reports of the Stevens Inquiry, it seems extraordinary that after eight months of investigation the report could have come to such a pathetic and uninspired conclusion.

Ever since the fire, Sir John Stevens has been convinced that the blaze in the RUC headquarters was the work of Military Intelligence. In his third report in 2003, he went as far as to say, 'This incident, in my opinion, has never been adequately investigated and I believe it was a deliberate act of arson.' He also claimed that army officers had done their best to frustrate his investigation from the beginning. For instance, Military Intelligence initially told the inquiry team that they did not run any agents; their role was simply to assist and to advise the RUC's Special Branch – they were lying through their teeth.

In retrospect, it seems extraordinary that Military Intelligence should have attempted to lie their way out of such questioning. They would have known that the Stevens team of detectives would eventually discover the truth of Military Intelligence's role in the undercover war against the paramilitary organisations. They were also aware that MI5 had briefed John Stevens and his senior officers on the undercover operations being carried out against the Provos. And, importantly, British Military Intelligence knew that MI5 were no friends of the Force Research Unit. Indeed, on many occasions MI5 tried to thwart the efforts of a number of FRU activities because they resented the fact the Force Research Unit had become a highly successful direct rival to MI5.

In time, the murder of Patrick Finucane would lead directly to other killings. The first was that of a Special Branch officer, Detective Chief Inspector David Murphy of Lurgan CID, who was shot dead while out duck shooting in Northern Ireland in November 1990. He was accompanied by three friends, Detective Constable George Taylor, 49, a Special Branch reserve constable, and two civilians, Norman Kendall, aged 44, a former member of the Ulster Defence Regiment (UDR), and Keith Dowey, 30, a civil servant. All four were Orangemen and members of the Point Gun Club. It was later claimed the four were shot dead by a Provo active service unit.

To those officers who knew David Murphy and George Taylor well, respected them as good, honest coppers and knew them to be tough and astute, the idea that two or three Provo gunmen would have been able to walk across an open field in broad daylight towards two Special Branch officers on a pheasant shoot, draw their guns and then shoot them dead seemed beyond belief.

Three of the men were keen members of the RUC Clay Pigeon Club and crack shots, and Keith Dowey was a guest. They could handle guns professionally and at speed. All four men had been wearing civilian clothes with no hint that two of them were police officers. At the time of the killings the officers were armed with shotguns and were also carrying their own personal side-arms. They had travelled to the shoot in one unmarked vehicle, a private car belonging to one of the men. The extraordinary shootings bore all the hallmarks of a cold-blooded killing and, according to forensic tests, the men were all shot at close quarters.

It is for these reasons that comrades in the RUC were of the opinion that they must have known their killers to permit them to get so close. Forensic tests also revealed that neither of the men had fired their side-arms and, indeed, neither had taken out, or seemingly attempted to take out, the handguns from their holsters.

Today, their colleagues in the RUC believe their killings were probably linked to the murder of Pat Finucane. Detective Chief Inspector Murphy had known Pat Finucane well and respected him. Their paths had crossed many times. Following Finucane's murder, DI Murphy had spent some months probing and investigating his killing. Murphy's friends have confirmed that he was the type of man who would not let sleeping dogs lie but would have sought to bring those responsible for Finucane's murder into the public domain so that justice could then take its course.

Today, with the Stevens Inquiry still in progress, there are some SB officers who are convinced the four men were killed because David Murphy had discovered who was responsible for Finucane's murder and, as a decent cop, he was against such cold-blooded killings organised by the security forces. Of course, MI5 would not have welcomed such intrusion into the plot that had been so carefully planned and put into operation. However, there are others who believe that not even MI5 would have ordered or condoned the killing of three innocent men simply because a keen SB officer was intent on revealing those responsible for Finucane's murder. They could easily have waited for another opportunity.

Another killing which represented yet another lethal twist in the Finucane saga was the murder of William Stobie in December 2001; he was shot dead 12 years after Finucane's killing. This author understands that those in the Stevens Inquiry team believe Stobie's killing was connected with Finucane's death.

The accepted theory is that Stobie was killed by members of the UDA because he was, by his own admission, an RUC Special Branch informer who passed on information about the inner workings of the UDA to his handlers. This had, indeed, been narrowed down further, the received wisdom being that 'C' Company of the UDA were responsible for the shooting of the tout.

But this purported reason for Stobie's killing is open to question, as there had always been a fairly close relationship between some members of the UDA and RUC Special Branch. Many members of the UDA and the SB were friends; many had been to the same schools and were members of the same Lodge; many shared relatives, attended the same parties, drank in the same pubs, worshipped in the same churches, supported the same soccer and rugby teams and enjoyed each other's company. They were all stalwart supporters of the Protestant and Unionist cause in Northern Ireland and, at heart, the great majority were Loyalists.

They fed each other tit-bits of information and intelligence over a pint of beer. In effect, they were working together in what they both assumed was a common cause.

Sir John Stevens' team uncovered the fact that Billy Stobie had been involved in Pat Finucane's murder but believed there were other dark forces involved besides Stobie, who had admitted being one of the UDA's quartermasters. The bald-headed Stobie confirmed that he had supplied UDA gunmen with the weapon used to kill Finucane and he had later got rid of it. As a result, Stobie was charged with conspiracy to murder and he also faced another charge of murdering Protestant teenager Adam Lambert in 1987. The case collapsed on a technicality, however, and Stobie walked out of Belfast Crown Court in November 2001 a free man. He may have been free but he knew in his heart that his days were numbered.

Fearing for his life, Stobie twice wrote to the Northern Ireland Office seeking to be included in the Government's Key Persons Protection Scheme (KPPS) – which gives practical and financial aid to those whose lives are thought to be at risk of paramilitary attack. Under the terms of the scheme, those under threat can be provided with assistance and advice. Approval by the KPPS could mean, for example, that a gun licence can be speedily arranged and training given in the use of the weapon, as well as advice in various ways of countering armed assailants. Some people qualify for extensive and expensive alterations to their homes, ranging from the fitting of bullet-proof windows to light-sensitive alarms and panic buttons which instantly relay an alarm to the nearest police station. Those considered to be under serious threat may also qualify to be re-housed, and in Stobie's case that should have been the immediate action that was taken.

And yet the Government never even acknowledged the letters, nor did they write back to Stobie or his solicitor. Stobie's second letter to the Northern Ireland Office requesting their help was sent only nine days before he was murdered. Indeed, after his death it was even claimed that he had turned down offers of protection.

A few days after Stobie walked free from court, he announced, somewhat surprisingly, that he would fully support an independent inquiry into Pat Finucane's murder. It was that single, simple statement that sealed Stobie's fate, for he most certainly knew the names and identities of those responsible for ordering Finucane's murder.

Urgent discussions took place in Belfast involving MI5 and Special Branch senior officers. They were well aware that Billy Stobie knew the names of those men who had been handed the task of killing Finucane and now they feared Stobie was on the verge of spilling the beans. Stobie's statement had changed everything. For those men in command of the intelligence agencies and the Special Branch it had become imperative to take out William Stobie to prevent him talking.

It was just six o'clock on the morning of Wednesday, 12 December 2001 when Stobie left his home – a flat in the mainly Protestant Forthriver Road in the Glencairn area of Belfast. Each weekday morning Stobie carried out the same routine while getting the car out to drive his partner to work. Stobie would walk to the car parked in the driveway and reverse it into the road. But waiting at the bottom of the drive that morning was a gunman who shot Stobie almost at point-blank range, killing him outright with five shots to the head and upper body. But who had fired those fatal shots and who had taken the decision to organise the shooting?

It is true to say that there were huge sighs of relief in many offices in Northern Ireland and London when the news came through of Stobie's death. The one person who could give damning evidence to an independent inquiry had been silenced.

On 17 April 2003, Sir John Stevens published a summary of his interim report in which he stated:

> I have uncovered enough evidence to lead me to believe that
> the murders of Patrick Finucane and Brian Adam Lambert

could have been prevented. I also believe that the RUC investigation of Patrick Finucane's murder should have resulted in the early arrest and detection of his killers.

I conclude there was collusion in both murders and the circumstances surrounding them. Collusion is evidenced in many ways. This ranges from the wilful failure to keep records, the absence of accountability, the withholding of intelligence and evidence, through to the extreme of agents being involved in murder.

At the time of writing, one man remains in custody charged with the murder of Patrick Finucane, but after 15 years of lies and the obstruction of investigations into his death it appears very unlikely that those actually responsible will ever be brought to justice.

Chapter Two

THE SILENT HUNTERS MOVE IN

The mounting complexity of the intelligence-gathering process since the late 1960s has been almost mesmerising, thanks primarily to the arrival in general use of the now-ubiquitous computer. But even in these high-tech days of complicated electronics and gizmos, satellite and aerial reconnaissance, those involved in the world of espionage understand that the most crucial part of intelligence work is still, as it has been for centuries, human intelligence or, in the parlance of the security services, 'HumInt'.

One of the principal problems facing today's intelligence services is not, in fact, lack of information but overkill. Material gathered via computers and other technical methods, such as sophisticated listening devices and phone tapping, requires long, intricate processing before any conclusions can be drawn. In the case of signals, which all intelligence services use, much is encoded and the codes are difficult and sometimes impossible to break. Overkill occurs when the quantity of incoming material exceeds the capacity of analysts to process it, causing a breakdown in their ability to make evaluations.

Indeed, most intelligence agencies are now forced to accept that between 80 and 90 per cent of intelligence gathered via computers and technical means is never processed. But pressure is still placed upon them to keep up with the latest technological developments, one important reason being that such means of obtaining intelligence do not involve risking the lives of operators on the ground. Human intelligence gathering is an extremely precarious pursuit and generates a comparatively small volume of information. But, even today, it continues to be the only way of obtaining certain kinds of information and is, generally speaking, more accurate.

Throughout the thirty years of the Troubles, three British intelligence services operated in Northern Ireland, assisted by numerous other undercover organisations which also played their part. The senior agency, of course, was MI5, known to one and all as 'Box' because their address, along with that of MI6, was a box number in London's Curzon Street. Second was the RUC Special Branch and third, the new team on the block, the Force Research Unit. The other organisations linked to the main intelligence agencies included E4A, the RUC's covert surveillance unit; the 'Det', military specialist surveillance units, more often than not SAS personnel detached from their own regiment, who worked closely with the 14th Intelligence Company, the covert surveillance unit within the RUC Special Branch. For each of these main agencies, as the security situation in the Province deteriorated, HumInt became a crucial factor as they struggled to gain the upper hand over the various terrorist organisations at work.

The intelligence services had been taken by surprise as the civil rights campaign in Northern Ireland slithered inexorably into divisive hate-filled trials of strength between the underprivileged Catholic minority and the ruling Protestant elite who ran the government, the civil service, the police, the emergency services, the courts and the great majority of the firms and businesses of

44

Northern Ireland. The Northern Ireland Civil Rights Association (NICRA) had been formed in February 1967 to demand a more equal and just society in the Province, making specific requests for universal suffrage, an end to discrimination against Catholics in the allocation of public-sector housing and in employment, the disbanding of the hated 'B Specials' police units and the repeal of the Special Powers Act. Inspired by similar movements in the United States and elsewhere, its members took to the streets in 1968 in what were intended to be peaceful protests, but they were met with increasingly violent opposition.

Throughout those crucial months of the late 1960s and early 1970s, the British Government did very little to intervene in the Province, holding its collective breath and hoping that the problem would eventually wither and die. But as they watched and waited, the peaceful demonstrations deteriorated into pitched battles with the RUC and its B Specials, who used their sticks and batons as they attempted to drive the campaigners off the streets with brute force.

This author witnessed at first hand the violent reaction to civil rights demonstrations, and in the majority of cases it appeared to be a heavy-handed overreaction to the campaigners' peaceful marches. Many mainland British viewers and the wider world watched with horror as images were relayed on their television screens of the brutal way in which the campaigners were being treated on the streets of the Province by thuggish, baton-wielding Northern Ireland policemen who resorted to the use of tear gas and violence. Overseas, the response was one of surprise and dismay that Britain, often regarded as the birthplace of democracy and free speech, a country the world looked up to as civilised and fair, could react with such hostility to peaceful demonstrators.

Blinkered politicians in mainland Britain, however, seemed only to see a Republican rabble defying the forces of law and order on the streets of Belfast and Derry, and they were urged by Ulster

Unionist politicians to assist in cracking down on the troublemakers who, they claimed, were hell-bent on reducing Belfast and Derry to rubble and ashes, destroying jobs, factories, shops and the Province's infrastructure. Eventually, after passing legislation in response to some of the protestors' demands, many in the Westminster Government felt they had no option but to support the authorities in Northern Ireland in every way possible, in a determined bid to defeat the uprising which seemed to threaten the very fabric of a part of the United Kingdom. They believed the best way to show their support was to send troops to Northern Ireland to quell the protestors, protect the Catholic minority and restore order on the streets. The Government believed that the army could quickly restore order and so, on 14 August 1969, as the Battle of the Bogside raged in Derry and began to spread to other towns, British troops arrived in the Province.

The reason the two governments were stumbling around in the dark with little or no idea of what was happening on the ground was an almost complete lack of meaningful intelligence. Neither the RUC nor the small British Army force initially sent to Northern Ireland had any intelligence briefings for the first few months simply because there was no up-to-date intelligence material to discuss. When the Troubles erupted into violence and the Northern Ireland civil rights campaign was hijacked by the Provisional IRA, the RUC's entire complement of Special Branch officers (then called Crime Special) amounted to just 20 people. And their experience in keeping a watching brief on the IRA had been directed solely at the old Official IRA; they had no knowledge whatsoever of the new young breed of Republicans who eventually emerged as the hardline Provisional IRA.

It was not until 1972 that the first team of MI5 agents was despatched to the Province. Until then, responsibility for the British Government's intelligence organisation rested with MI6, Britain's Secret Intelligence Service, which had mainly been confined to political operations in the Republic. It was MI6 that was responsible for setting up the arms deal that led to the trial of the Irish government ministers Charles Haughey and Neil Blaney. In 1970, the ministers were dismissed by the Taoiseach for allegedly using government money to import arms for the IRA. Though both were acquitted, their departure from the Cabinet weakened Nationalist support.

MI6 was finally given its marching orders from Northern Ireland following the fiasco surrounding the Littlejohn brothers. This MI6 operation was deemed to be so naively planned and executed that MI5 seized the opportunity to take over responsibility for Northern Ireland, leaving MI6 to continue watching the Republic. The Littlejohn brothers, Kenneth and Keith, had been taken on by MI6 as undercover agents and urged to act as agent provocateurs, briefed to infiltrate and inform on the Official IRA as well as organising and carrying out bank robberies and bomb attacks in the Republic for which, it was anticipated, the Official IRA would be blamed. It was hoped that this would lead to an anti-Republican backlash. The career of the Littlejohns as MI6 agents came to an embarrassing conclusion after they raided the Allied Irish Bank in Grafton Street, Dublin, in October 1972, holding the manager's family at gunpoint and getting away with £67,000. Having left their fingerprints all over the place, they were arrested on the mainland seven days later. Eventually, after discussions between British and Irish officials, the Littlejohn brothers were extradited to Ireland, tried, found guilty and sentenced to heavy jail terms: 20 years for Kenneth and 15 years for Keith.

The Littlejohn affair had severe repercussions for Britain's intelligence services. Some 20 MI6 field officers in both the Six Counties and the Republic had to be removed, and authority for all intelligence matters in the Province was passed exclusively to MI5.

The newly arrived MI5 team were shocked to discover that the

RUC Special Branch had not a single address of any high-ranking Republican, Sinn Fein leader or IRA officer. And, in most cases, the names and addresses of IRA men they did have were out of date. Indeed, some of those Official IRA members on the RUC list had, in fact, died; others had not attended an IRA meeting for years. Some had moved house ten years previously.

In discussions with senior officers of MI5, government ministers accepted their initial analysis, gleaned from MI6, that there was no quick fix to the desperate situation in the Province. Senior MI5 officers informed Northern Ireland ministers that they were aware that the Provos were smuggling arms, ammunition and Semtex into Ireland and burying them in dumps in the South. They were setting up camps in which to train young men to handle and fire various weapons, ranging from AK-47s to any handguns they could find. They were also teaching some volunteers the skills of bomb making. As a result of such findings, MI5 concluded that the only way to defeat the IRA had become a long haul, and one of the few ways of achieving that aim would be to recruit dozens, if not scores, of informants from the Catholic minority so that they could organise the defeat of the IRA with the help of their own sympathisers and, if possible, from within their own ranks.

The new MI5 senior officers spent the next two years reorganising the RUC, moulding it into a 6,000-strong paramilitary force equipped with high-velocity weapons, riot-control gear and vehicles, creating a Special Patrol Group and establishing a large Special Branch wing tasked with setting up and training a team of newly recruited handlers to encourage young Catholics to become police informers and, hopefully, to one day infiltrate the Republican movement to provide high-grade intelligence. MI5 had judged, correctly, that politicians and senior police and army officers could only carry out their duty of restoring peace to the streets of Northern Ireland if they were provided with meaningful intelligence on which to base their policies. Without such intelligence, they were simply working in the dark with little or no hope of targeting and arresting the troublemakers who were hell-bent on escalating the protests to full-scale civil strife.

Understandably, the creation of an efficient intelligence-gathering unit within the RUC Special Branch, with reliable and good informants, took a number of years. There was a long history of hostility between the Catholic population and the RUC, and attracting young, out-of-work Catholic teenagers who were happy to take the RUC shilling was made even more difficult by the fact that, by 1973, RUC patrols had all but ceased in Catholic areas as a result of the escalating number of attacks against officers. Local 'policing' had been taken over by the Provos, who jumped at the chance to act as the unofficial authoritative force within those no-go areas when the RUC withdrew their foot patrols. They enjoyed their new-found status and responsibilities, and some brutish PIRA zealots ruthlessly exploited their power, inflicting beatings in an effort to stamp their authority on those they purported to protect.

It was not just the IRA who were stepping up their activities. From the mid-1970s onwards, sectarian murders became the order of the day in the Province, with both the UDA and the UVF heavily involved in dozens of attacks and some killings. These attacks would continue on and off for a generation, though it was always heavily denied at every political level that the UDA and the UVF were involved. It was more often than not claimed that internecine warfare within the ranks of the Official IRA and the Provos was responsible for the killings, despite the fact there was little or no supporting evidence. In true British style, these killings were simply brushed under the carpet as though they had never happened.

At first, indeed, behind closed doors, the British Government appeared to welcome the arrival of Loyalists paramilitaries as a third force, striking terror into Catholic areas in a bid to destabilise the IRA support. These ad hoc mobs of Loyalist men of violence became involved in the killings of Catholics and not necessarily those Catholics who were members of a Republican organisation, the IRA or any of the other Nationalist forces. The Loyalists were granted virtual, though unofficial, immunity to carry out their acts of violence. RUC and army patrols were kept out of districts which the Loyalists planned to attack, roads were left open for them and weapons searches were rarely undertaken in Loyalist areas. And even elements within the British Army became involved in the disgraceful one-sided chicanery, for senior army officers, with the unofficial nod from the Government, went about the business of striking terror into Catholic areas, including through the killings of several decent, ordinary Catholics with no known IRA connection. This conspiracy between British Military Intelligence and the gunmen of the UDA was sanctioned at the highest level of the British Government and was first revealed by this author in the book *Ten-Thirty-Three*.

As surprising as it may now sound, the first British troops to patrol the streets of Northern Ireland in 1969 had actually been welcomed by many members of the Nationalist Catholic community, as they believed the soldiers had come to offer them some protection from the Loyalist attacks on their homes and communities. These often inexperienced soldiers faced a difficult task, however, as they were not only asked to stop the fighting and police the areas of violent confrontation between the two communities but were also expected to gather information about IRA suspects as they went about their daylight duty of patrolling the streets. They had little, if any, local knowledge and, as a result, the information they did gather was negligible and, more often than not, useless.

In a rather naive effort to improve intelligence gathering, the Ministry of Defence, on advice from MI5, encouraged the troops to adopt a policy of 'tea and sympathy', whereby squaddies would be urged to stop and chat with the locals during their patrols in an effort to gain the confidence of ordinary Catholics, win their support by their kindly attitude and, hopefully, learn some useful information. However, not unsurprisingly, this policy produced no substantial intelligence and as the Provos gained ever more control of Republican areas, British soldiers became their prime targets. The 'tea and sympathy' policy had to be dropped.

The IRA was determined to tarnish the reputation of the British Army in the eyes of their supporters, the downtrodden Catholic minority. The Provos wanted the soldiers to be seen as an army of occupation that was suppressing the Irish people. In these efforts they were given plenty of ammunition by the less than admirable actions taken by one of the army's elite groups – the SAS.

The story of the Special Air Service in Northern Ireland and, indeed, in the Republic of Ireland has never been fully revealed. Most of what can be described as 'official' SAS history maintains that the first SAS units went to Northern Ireland in 1969 under the fig-leaf pretence of preventing gun running by Loyalist paramilitaries, and it was not until the 1970s that their activities were stepped up. The official line at the time was that the SAS remained in Northern Ireland in 1969 only for a short time and were then withdrawn and re-introduced as shock troops in January 1976 by Prime Minister Harold Wilson for three main reasons. First, figures had been released showing the IRA were inflicting heavy casualties among the British Army troops stationed in the Province and it was seen as imperative that this situation be reversed. Second, the Wilson Government hoped that introducing the hard men of the SAS onto the streets of Belfast and Derry in particular might help to subdue the rising passions on both sides of the sectarian divide. Third, the British Government hoped that the unique SAS training could be used to devastating effect against the Provos in south Armagh, which had become the IRA's fiefdom, training ground and arms dump in Northern Ireland after they had forced the RUC to pull out. Prime Minister Wilson also hoped that the tough no-nonsense tactics would be sufficient to quell the rising tide of violence they believed was being whipped up by the Catholic minority in support of their civil rights campaign.

Importantly, after many appeals from the Ulster Unionists, the British Government also wanted to placate the growing unease of the Protestant majority by acting decisively. Sending in the SAS was seen as a good political move to show that the Westminster Government was determined to stamp out the fermenting civil conflict.

Once there, however, for most of the 30 years of strife there were always at least a few SAS troops on duty in the Province, mainly in small units operating undercover in civilian clothes, sometimes on detachment as part of the 14th Intelligence Company with whom they operated. Another SAS responsibility throughout the 30 years of the Troubles was to patrol south Armagh – nicknamed 'bandit country'. Throughout the Troubles, south Armagh and the desolate, open border region was used as an active-service training ground for the SAS but it was also here that one or two SAS 'bricks' would spend weeks at a time searching for Provo activists whom they hoped to intercept in the act of bringing arms and ammunition into the north from their dumps in the Republic. There was also a semi-permanent troop or two of SAS soldiers stationed at RAF Aldergrove, ready with their own dedicated helicopters to be airlifted to anywhere in the Province, literally at a moment's notice.

One of the men responsible for urging the introduction of SAS troops in Northern Ireland was the tough, no-nonsense Brigadier Frank Kitson, who served as Army Commander in Belfast from the spring of 1970 to April 1972. He had previously served in Kenya, Muscat and Oman, and Cyprus. He brought with him a wealth of experience in counter-insurgency, which he put into practice in Northern Ireland. Kitson had been renowned for his ruthless approach to putting down the Mau Mau insurgents in Kenya and it has been suggested that Kitson adopted a similar pattern of control in Northern Ireland: using the MRF – Mobile Reaction Forces – often with SAS men or warrant officers in command of small units, to carry out killings and dirty-tricks operations against the IRA.

It has been alleged that the escalation of violent action by the forces of law and order accelerated dramatically during Kitson's two-year stay in the Province. Harassment, arrests, brutality and torture, internment, long prison sentences, house-wrecking and selected killings went on apace in a bid to break the morale of the Catholics. But such treatment only seemed to invigorate them, forcing the Nationalists to protect their homes and neighbourhoods against attack. The result was often rioting and, later, bombings and shootings, as the IRA stepped up its campaign, offering protection to Catholic families on Republican estates who were the target not only of wayward gangs of Loyalist paramilitaries but also the RUC and, on occasions, units of the British Army. To permit this state of affairs to occur and persist was one of the British Government's most serious mistakes, for the entire Catholic population came to believe the Westminster Government was on the side of the Protestant majority and that they viewed the Catholic minority as the enemy.

The tactics of the army, notably members of the SAS and the Royal Marine Commandos, were listed by Father Denis Faul in a case he put before the European Commission of Human Rights after interviews with Catholic families in south Armagh. The alleged brutalities included beating people with rifle butts, kicking and thumping local residents, death threats, simulated executions, attempted suffocations, night-time assaults on isolated farmhouses and the psychological torture of old-age pensioners.

Prior to the first SAS troops being despatched to the Province, the initial training for their mission, which took place in England, involved interrogation techniques, the organisation and running of military quick-reaction forces, and, finally, tactics for and methods of dealing with armed gangs. Nothing was included about techniques for disarming gun-running Loyalists or dissuading and stopping the brutish young 'Prods' from attacking and burning Catholic homes.

Within months of the first SAS troops arriving in Northern

Ireland, reports began to filter out of alleged torture being carried out on IRA suspects if they refused to cooperate with their captors. The soldiers wanted information – names and addresses of IRA suspects. When the SAS discovered that the Catholic population didn't want to provide this information of their own free will, or, as they would have viewed it, didn't want to betray their kith and kin, the SAS were given the go-ahead to attempt more direct, more ruthless means of persuasion.

When suspects didn't crack under intense interrogation, it became known that some SAS troops would go further in their efforts to extract information. On some occasions, victims alleged their heads were covered in hoods and they were kicked and beaten; others told of being ordered to stand facing a wall using only their fingertips for support, sometimes for 24 hours at a stretch. Others complained that they were subjected to another torture technique: forced to listen to a sustained high-pitched noise for hours at a time which made sleep impossible and sometimes reduced victims to nervous, shaking wrecks. The IRA described these torture techniques as the new method of SAS intelligence gathering.

The British Government were pleased with the results from such interrogation methods, for within three years, 1970–3, over 2,000 Provos were imprisoned. Ultimately, however, these interrogation methods proved counter-productive, as the stories of those subjected to such inhumane interrogation circulated in the Catholic clubs and pubs of Northern Ireland. Though it was usually the Special Branch, aided by the RUC, who carried out such interrogations, having learned the techniques from the SAS, the Provos blamed the hated and feared SAS for introducing the torture techniques. As a result, the SAS became the Provos' number-one enemy and were hated by the Catholic population for their inhuman treatment of their fathers, sons and husbands.

To the SAS, however, these methods of deep interrogation were perfectly acceptable. In their tough training schedules, those aspiring to join the exclusive elite regiment went through very similar ordeals in case they had to survive such treatment if ever captured in countries where such questioning was simply a standard part of interrogation before other forms of torture were tried.

Reports of the brutality inflicted by the SAS were collated by Cardinal Conway, the Catholic Bishop of Armagh, and passed to the Ministry of Home Affairs in Northern Ireland in 1974. Amnesty International had first reported torture, allegedly by members of the SAS, against detainees in Northern Ireland in 1972 and this was followed by a more substantive report by the European Commission of Human Rights in 1976, with allegations of torture. The Commission found the British Government guilty of violating Article 3 of the European Convention on Human Rights on two counts and, as a result, new methods of questioning had to be adopted by the SAS, the RUC and the other security services.

Despite these complaints to the Commission, one year later, in 1977, the SAS was given a new brief to step up undercover operations in Belfast, Derry and south Armagh. The then Army Minister, Robert Brown, gave a written answer to the House of Commons, stating:

> The SAS has had a significant effect in reducing terrorist activity in the rural and border areas of south Armagh. It has, therefore, been decided that their skills and the experience gained will be used, where appropriate, in other similarly troubled areas.

In effect, this was the green light giving the go-ahead for the SAS to roam around Northern Ireland dressed in civilian clothes and armed with handguns and/or sub-machine guns. The idea was that this would instil fear into the hearts of the IRA.

Towards the end of 1977, the SAS began a rather bizarre form of secret warfare in the Province. At different times they would set off explosions in border areas to create confusion; they also planted ammunition on suspects and in their cars, and left false trails leading to men considered possible IRA suspects. Some SAS soldiers in civilian clothes even posed as pressmen or photographers to gain access to Nationalist areas of Belfast and Derry. But this rum form of warfare was quietly dropped with the arrival of the avuncular Sir Maurice Oldfield.

Sir Maurice, the former Director-General of the Secret Intelligence Service in London, was appointed to the job of coordinating the work of the SAS in the different units of the British Army and with the RUC by Margaret Thatcher within weeks of her becoming Prime Minister in 1979.

With a staff of 40 top-flight intelligence officers, Sir Maurice was also responsible for the introduction of 'screening', the highly successful method later adopted by the Force Research Unit in their efforts to woo members of the Catholic community into working undercover as agents on behalf of the British Army. Within 18 months of Sir Maurice Oldfield's arrival in Belfast, some 30 informers had provided evidence which led to the arrest of more than 300 suspected terrorists. IRA bombings were reduced in number and terrorist killings were halved within two years. The FRU refined the screening process to a fine art and many agents, including the celebrated super-spy Steak Knife, were recruited by this gentle process of persuasion and financial reward.

The election victory of Margaret Thatcher in 1979 increased the impetus behind the British Government's determination to 'smash' Republican terror groups. Ever since the 1979 murder of her close friend Airey Neave, Mrs Thatcher had been determined to use her power and influence when she became Prime Minister to hunt down the killers. The fight against the Republican terrorists was made all the more difficult at this time by the fact that, by the early 1980s, the Provisional IRA had adopted the cell system. The IRA had been reorganised on a regional basis, with volunteers from each brigade – Belfast, Derry, Border, etc. – working in autonomous active service units of no more than six members. Different phases of each operation – obtaining vehicles, moving weapons, making bombs – were now carried out by different units which had no designated fixed areas within the brigade region. The cell system had been adopted by many European terrorist gangs involved in urban and guerrilla warfare because of the protection it offered those involved. Members of the cell only knew each other's identities, not those of the members of other groups, and only the leader had access to a commander. This system meant it was very hard for any undercover agents to penetrate the cells and provide intelligence about their planned actions.

Such problems were not going to deter a woman with Margaret Thatcher's iron will, however, and nor did the infamous October 1984 IRA attack on the Grand Hotel in Brighton.

The attack on the hotel where the annual Conservative Party Conference was being held nearly cut a swathe through the members of the Cabinet and was one of the IRA's most audacious attacks. Mrs Thatcher escaped injury but the explosion trapped and injured a number of Tory MPs and their wives, and resulted in the deaths of Sir Anthony Berry MP, Roberta Wakeham (the wife of the government chief whip), Jeanne Shattock, Eric Taylor and Muriel MacLean (the wife of Donald MacLean, a senior figure in the Scottish Conservative Party). From then on, Thatcher would use all the powers at her command to defeat Republican terrorism.

As a result of that single bomb blast in Brighton, the great majority of Britain's leaders in all fields, from politics to the City, suddenly realised that the affairs of Northern Ireland had changed forever and that what was going on in Northern Ireland had to be addressed and quickly. By the time of the Brighton bombing ordinary people throughout England, Wales and Scotland had come to the realisation that the Provisional IRA were not do-gooders demanding civil rights for the Catholic minority of

Northern Ireland but, rather, a group of ruthless and determined terrorists using the bomb and the bullet indiscriminately to achieve their political ends. Their political goal was the coercion of the majority of the people of Northern Ireland, who had demonstrated their wish to remain part of the United Kingdom, into an all-Ireland state.

Mrs Thatcher was determined to stop them getting their way and, as a result of the Brighton bombing, she now had the vast majority of voters on her side. They realised the Provos had to be stopped and, in effect, gave carte blanche to the Government to do whatever was necessary to bring an end to the Provos' campaign of killings and bombings.

Within days of the Brighton security breakdown, Mrs Thatcher, as chairman of the Joint Intelligence Committee which met weekly at Downing Street, ordered a complete review of the security and intelligence set-up in Northern Ireland to ensure that such a mistake would never be repeated. She held MI5 to account for the security failings and never again did she have real faith in that security service. Indeed, in a private meeting with MI5 chiefs following the Brighton bombing, an angry Mrs Thatcher accused them of carrying out their duties like 'incompetent amateurs'. The Prime Minister was not only critical of MI5's lack of success in Northern Ireland but she also seemed to be of the opinion that the whole structure of MI5 and its agents were simply not capable of providing reliable intelligence on the Province, its politicians, the IRA, the Loyalists or the security background. Mrs Thatcher believed that MI5 personnel were not sufficiently rigorous and down-to-earth to cope with the hardmen of the IRA and the Loyalist terror groups. She believed they were simply of a different breed to those they had to deal with in the Province. She found the MI5 men too civil, too refined and too sensitive for the tough tasks facing them.

Mrs Thatcher had more faith in Britain's Military Intelligence machine and she encouraged British Military Intelligence to set up research offices in Northern Ireland as an additional intelligence service to MI5. In 1981, the Force Research Unit had been officially established and Mrs Thatcher now urged Military Intelligence to take an even more proactive role against the Provos. She wanted action and, more importantly, she wanted results.

With Thatcher's support, money began pouring in to the Force Research Unit. New and better cars were provided, the latest and most sophisticated weapons were purchased, training was increased and officers and handlers were encouraged to undertake SAS training at Hereford. She also encouraged Military Intelligence to scour other security services to recruit the brightest and best to join the Force Research Unit. Senior NCOs and warrant officers of the highest calibre were recruited and set the task of undermining and, if possible, crushing the Provisional IRA.

The men recruited, all volunteers to the new unit, were withdrawn from mainstream barracks and housed separately in their own secure offices and compounds, or quartered in safe houses. The FRU also had its own administration section, transport depot and clerks. The personnel were given good salaries as well as generous expense accounts. Overnight, the FRU had become an elite intelligence unit which would later come to rival the intelligence-gathering capability of MI5 in the Province.

Mrs Thatcher understood that the RUC Special Branch had encountered real difficulty in recruiting touts from the Catholic minority because of the decades of animosity between the majority Protestant RUC and the Catholic minority. Despite the fact that the initial good relationship between the Catholics and the British Army had broken down, Thatcher and her advisers believed it was worth setting up a Military Intelligence organisation in the hope that they, with their professional training as intelligence officers, might be able to encourage enough young Catholics to work for them.

In fact, the RUC had earlier come up with a similar screening process, in which young, cash-strapped Catholic lads were brought into local RUC stations as though they were being taken in for questioning. The lads found officers friendly and chatty, seemingly wanting to make them feel at ease. There was only one problem. The lads could not be seen walking into RUC stations because of the hostility the Catholic population of Northern Ireland had always felt towards the hated Protestant-dominated police force. So, as soon as the lads agreed to help, they were treated like any other tout and clandestine arrangements were made for interviews. The FRU was now encouraged to develop this process and the need for accurate intelligence soon became more urgent than ever.

The signing of the Anglo-Irish Agreement in November 1985 changed the political reality in the Province. The British Government had not only agreed to redress Catholic grievances concerning the administration of justice in the Six Counties but had also agreed that the Irish Government could play a role in Northern Ireland and establish a secretariat at Maryfield, County Down, permitting Irish officials to oversee certain aspects of the Province. Protestant politicians and the Loyalist community at large were outraged.

The agreement galvanised Ulster Defence Association chiefs into action, for they had come to the conclusion that they could no longer rely on the RUC or the British Army to protect the Protestant majority, particularly in the country areas. As a result they had decided to create a military wing of some strength and within a matter of months the UDA and the UVF – the Ulster Volunteer Force – took the law into their own hands. During the following decade, the number of sectarian killings by Loyalists rose dramatically until they were killing more people than the Provos.

For the intelligence services, this breakdown in trust between the forces of law and order and the Loyalists was a disaster. Almost overnight, the cooperation between the RUC and the Loyalist paramilitaries had all but ceased and so had the intelligence material passing between them. Never again would the Loyalists put their trust in the Westminster Government, the RUC or the British Army.

As the weeks became months, the mood on the streets of Belfast and Derry deteriorated dramatically, mainly because the Loyalists had decided once again to go on the attack. Within a matter of months, the security services had no idea where the Loyalist paramilitaries would strike next. The RUC and the army were desperately playing catch-up and people were dying on the streets. The authorities needed details of the Loyalist organisations' personnel, finance, planning and, above all, the availability of weapons, ammunition, Semtex and detonators. And no such intelligence was coming in.

The TCG feared the situation was spiralling out of control and the problem, as ever, was a near-total lack of good intelligence. Added to this embarrassment was political pressure from London. The FRU, the RUC Special Branch and the Joint Irish Section – which comprised senior intelligence officers headed by a senior MI5 officer – were put under increasing political pressure to find reliable sources who would produce accurate up-to-date information about the Loyalist paramilitaries and the political strategy behind the actions of the hardline Protestants.

It was now that Mrs Thatcher's decision to back the Force Research Unit and put faith in a new breed of intelligence-gatherers paid off, leading to the Prime Minister putting even greater faith in Military Intelligence. Two undercover agents arrived on the scene, both working for the Force Research Unit, and became over time two of the most crucial elements in the British Government's war against the Provos as well as the successful infiltration of hardline Loyalist organisations. It added power to Mrs Thatcher's contention that MI5 weren't up to the job when she was told that the two undercover agents had in fact been stolen by the FRU from under the noses of MI5.

Throughout Mrs Thatcher's tenure at No. 10 Downing Street, British Military Intelligence and the Force Research Unit knew very well that they had the full backing of the Prime Minister in their efforts to track down and arrest, or flush out and kill, members of the Provisional IRA. And that gave them so much confidence that they too began to cut corners, sometimes working too closely with their agents, on occasions becoming dangerously close to colluding with them over their nefarious activities which increasingly involved the targeting and killing of known Provo activists.

Since Thatcher was ousted by her Cabinet ministers, both her successors, John Major and Tony Blair, have sought a path to peace and British Military intelligence gathering in Northern Ireland has become almost quiescent.

Thatcher's unequivocal support was the real reason British Military Intelligence were so cavalier when first answering questions put to them by the Stevens Inquiry team. Indeed, despite threats of arrest and prosecution for failing to comply with the inquiry's request for documents, the army's intelligence department dragged its heels for over 13 years before finally handing over its files and records to the inquiry team. Even then, some documents were still retained by British Military Intelligence until all were finally handed over in 2003.

And yet, despite all the hundreds of files and the thousands of reports written during the Troubles by the intelligence services, by far and away the single most vital element during the past three decades was HumInt, and so it was proved in spectacular fashion with the recruitment of Freddie Scappaticci, who came to work at the very heart of the Provisional IRA, and, to a lesser degree, Brian Nelson, who worked as the chief intelligence officer of the Ulster Defence Association. For their part, the security services put such great emphasis on protecting those two secret intelligence sources that they were prepared to kill people if there was the slightest chance that these sources might be compromised. That must be borne in mind to fully comprehend the vital and dramatic part these sources played in saving and safeguarding the lives of many people not only in Northern Ireland but also on the mainland.

Chapter Three

STEAK KNIFE

In May 2003, newspaper headlines throughout the UK trumpeted the exposure of the most important agent ever recruited by the FRU in Northern Ireland: 'Named: British double agent who murdered for the IRA'; 'He did the IRA's dirty work for 25 years – and was paid £80,000 a year'; 'Street shocked as neighbour named as spy and torturer'. In revelations that apparently sent shockwaves through the ranks of the Provisional IRA, west Belfast man Freddie Scappaticci was unmasked as the agent codenamed 'Steak Knife', a spy said to have infiltrated the top echelons of the Republican terrorist organisation in order to provide intelligence for the security services. During the 1980s and '90s, senior Provo leaders had suspected that there might be a mole in their midst who was secretly working for the British Government, but none was discovered, no link unearthed. The conclusion was therefore drawn that the existence of such a spy was simply a rumour generated by British Intelligence to confuse and unnerve the Provisional IRA.

But the rumour was true. Steak Knife was real, and his name

was indeed Freddie Scappaticci, known for more than two decades by many senior Provos, including Gerry Adams with whom he was interned in 1971, as 'Scap'. He was a trusted member of the organisation and worked for the PIRA's internal security department as their chief interrogator. Scap's job was to question and, if necessary, torture those volunteers who had allegedly supplied information to the police or security services. In the eyes of the Provos, such men and women were traitors to the cause, despicable individuals who deserved the ultimate punishment. If they confessed to the charges, the penalty was always death, usually from a bullet in the back of the head.

Scap never actually pulled the trigger, but he employed the most macabre and horrifying methods to break his victims' morale and force them to confess their treachery. And yet, to all who knew him, Scap appeared the most inoffensive of men.

Freddie Scappaticci was born into an Italian immigrant family in Belfast in the late 1940s. He grew up with all the other young Catholic kids of west Belfast, coming of age in the days of heightened tension in the 1960s. During his young teenage years he had shared his fellow Catholics' feelings of rejection by the Protestant community, witnessed the humiliation of their parents by Protestant employers and the way they were forced to live as second-class citizens in their own country. He quickly came to understand that all the best jobs, whether in the private or the public sector, always seemed to go to Protestants and, in particular, Loyalists who belonged to the various Orange Lodges. As he grew older he saw for himself that the best houses on the smartest estates around Belfast were always occupied by Protestants.

He had also witnessed first-hand the way that RUC officers on the beat treated Catholic kids quite differently from the way they treated Protestant teenagers. While the Catholics frequently received a good belt around the ear and sometimes a good thumping, allegedly for giving cheek, he had never seen 'Prod' kids treated like that.

Like the majority of other young Catholic lads, he came to understand the anger and frustration felt by the adults of his community and he felt himself to be one of them. But Freddie Scappaticci was one of the luckier youngsters in Belfast, because his Italian parents and their Italian friends and relations had worked the Belfast fruit and vegetable markets for some 50 years, and he had grown up secure in the knowledge that when he left school there was a ready-made job for him helping to run the family business. From a young age, Freddie had helped various Italian families in the markets, fetching and carrying, running errands and stacking the shelves of their fruit and vegetable stalls. And when his parents opened a fish and chip shop, he readily lent a hand.

Most of his pals had only a life on the dole to look forward to, trying to scratch out a living in whatever way possible, sometimes getting work humping bricks on building sites, or some other form of manual labour, and all for low wages. Many young Catholic teenagers in Belfast at this time were earning their money thieving and shoplifting, as the unemployment rate amongst Catholics was so high. They would usually form a gang of perhaps three or four and then scout the shops they were going to rob while formulating a plan of action. Armed with whatever they had managed to steal, the lads would then tour the housing estates, going from door to door, attempting to sell their ill-gotten goods for cash. Most of the articles were clothes and they sold much of the gear at half-price. As a result, they earned quite good money, but it was not uncommon for them to be caught by the police. Some would be let off with a caution from a magistrate, but others, if they were repeat offenders, might find themselves placed in a home for some weeks to cool their heels. The older ones were usually jailed for a few months in an attempt to teach them a lesson. But they would later be released back onto the streets with no prospect of finding a legitimate job.

The first whispers of a civil rights movement in Northern Ireland could be heard in the 1960s. And Freddie, a bright, intelligent lad, identified strongly with what he saw and heard on his black-and-white television, for as he watched the scenes being broadcast from America of blacks being harassed, beaten and dragged away by the police while demonstrating for their civil rights, he recognised that for decades – if not centuries – the Catholics of Northern Ireland had been treated in the same way by the majority Protestant population. As far as he could see, there was little difference between the demands being made by black Americans and those of Northern Ireland Catholics.

With his Catholic teenage friends, Freddie became an enthusiastic participant in the civil rights marches and demonstrations that were a common feature of life in Northern Ireland in the late '60s, shouting the slogans with the rest of his friends because he wanted to be identified with them, wanted to be accepted as one of them. The Scappaticcis, like many immigrant families, had made few Irish friends, preferring to remain within the small, tight-knit Italian community, speaking their own language, continuing their traditional Italian customs rather than mixing with the native locals. Freddie, in contrast, had always wanted to be one of the Northern Ireland Catholic kids, to feel like he belonged as a member of their boyhood gangs.

The Northern Ireland civil rights campaign gave Freddie Scappaticci the chance to prove not only that he was one of them, supporting their cause, but also that he had the guts to join in the youthful protests, hurling not only insults but also stones and bottles at the hated police. Whatever the other Catholic lads of the Falls Road did to push forward their cause, hassle the police and disrupt the peace, Freddie Scappaticci was prepared to do the same. Indeed, Freddie earned his spurs during those first few years of the campaign, though his parents and the rest of his family were unaware that their hard-working teenage lad was spending his evenings taunting the RUC and throwing stones and bottles during pitched street battles.

On many occasions, Freddie witnessed some of his mates getting clobbered when an RUC officer managed to grab one of them in the hurly-burly of the confrontations and administer a few swift hard kicks and baton blows to teach the lad a lesson. Then came a night Freddie would never forget, when, aged sixteen, he was grabbed and beaten by three policemen during a mêlée in west Belfast. He was punched and kicked that summer night and received some hard, sharp blows from truncheons, but it was also the night that he won the respect of his former school pals. From then on, young Freddie was truly accepted as one of them and that acceptance changed his life.

Almost overnight, Freddie Scappaticci grew up. Now he took an even greater interest in the civil rights movement. He read and happily distributed their pamphlets, attended their meetings, listened to their speeches and took part in as many civil rights marches and demonstrations as he could. He had never before experienced such emotions or felt so passionate about a cause. Indeed, Scap would later tell his handlers that he became a young firebrand, always keen for action, eager to push the battle further than the other kids. He seemed to take ever-greater risks than his pals in taunting the RUC officers, and could frequently be found at the forefront of the action, hurling the bricks and stones harder than most and with increasing accuracy. As a result, Scap or 'Scapi' – as his young friends invariably called him – became a target for the RUC officers who came to see him as a ringleader.

Sometimes, on his own, Scap would spend his free time in target practice, hurling bricks and bottles at trees and other objects so that he developed a right arm both powerful and accurate. He prided himself that he could aim at a particular RUC officer and hit the target nine times out of ten. He then scaled down the size of the target so that later he would be able to hit the heads of officers from a fair distance, a display of accuracy which won the admiration of his mates who turned out with increasing frequency whenever protests took place behind the makeshift barricades thrown up in the streets where they lived.

Freddie worked hard by day and in the evenings, helping his parents in the fish and chip shop. But on the nights that demonstrations were planned, Scap would leave the shop early to make contact with his mates, looking forward in eager anticipation to the rioting and demonstrating, excited and inspired by the thought of what lay ahead. For Scap and his friends were still ordinary young lads: though they believed in the ideals of the civil rights movement, their taunting of RUC officers, rioting and demonstrating, setting up barricades and stealing and burning vehicles was treated like a sport as well as a deliberate act of political defiance.

In 1969, however, the sectarian tension in Northern Ireland escalated dramatically when the traditional August Apprentice Boys' march through Derry, which passed close to the Catholic Bogside area, resulted in riots that became known as the Battle of the Bogside. The unrest spread to Belfast and hundreds of Catholics' houses were burned, leaving many homeless. As a result, on 14 August, British Army troops were deployed to assist the RUC in restoring order to the Province.

Like the majority of the Catholic community, Scap initially welcomed the arrival of the British troops in Northern Ireland because he believed they had been deployed to protect the Catholic community from attacks by Loyalist gangs and from the beatings handed out by the RUC and the hated B Specials. Scap had no idea that the growing number of younger hard-line members of the IRA, who, late in 1969, broke away from the older Official organisation to form the Provisional IRA, had no wish for the Catholic community to become friendly with the British troops. As previously explained, the Provos wanted the downtrodden Catholic community to see the soldiers as an invading and occupying army which had no wish to assist or help them but had been despatched to Northern Ireland to sustain the status quo – to ensure Britain retained control of Northern Ireland and all its subjects.

The Provos were hell-bent on seizing the moment provided by the wave of civil rights demands surging through America and other parts of the world. They were determined to use this moment in history to persuade the Catholic community to rise up against the hated colonialist British Government. Their stated and understandable aim was the same as all the other Irish Republicans who had taken up arms against the Brits throughout the previous 70 years: to rid Ireland of the British and create a single, one-nation Ireland.

With their music and their songs of bravery and courage, the Republican clubs throughout Northern Ireland once again fostered anti-British sentiment and propaganda, and incited their members to take up arms for the cause. And, as ever, the Republicans appealed to their innocent young, the easily led teenagers, to take to the streets and the barricades. The young Catholic lads rose to the occasion with hot-headed enthusiasm, naivety and courage, urged on by their political leaders who had no wish to expose themselves to the truncheons of the RUC or the batons of the British troops.

Within a matter of a few weeks, the demonstrations that would previously have ended at 3 a.m. with the British troops and the young demonstrators declaring the rioting a friendly draw had changed dramatically. The sticks and stones gave way to petrol bombs and gunfire, and the camaraderie that had existed between the two sides was replaced with a burgeoning and real hostility. Over a period of a few months, the same feelings of hatred and loathing that had been reserved for the RUC were now aimed at the occupying British troops. Encouraged by their Provo leaders, the young, enthusiastic lads in Derry and west Belfast came to view the British Army as a hateful enemy to be challenged on the streets, made to feel unwelcome and attacked with every piece of weaponry that came to hand. The civil strife that was to consume Northern Ireland over the following 30 years, leading on occasions almost to a state of civil war, had begun in earnest.

Not only did Freddie Scappaticci find himself at the very heart of this bitter internecine war, but he was also at the centre of the battle for power that raged for several months between the hot-blooded young Provos, who wanted action on the streets, and the older, more conservative Official IRA, who believed a political solution could be achieved without the need for bloodshed.

At this time at the end of the decade, Freddie knew men on both sides of this divide. He respected the older Officials not only because he associated age with wisdom but also because of their experience of earlier trials of strength against the forces of law and order. However, Freddie's youthful energy and passion for the cause eventually drove him to support the young activists – his school friends, who seemed prepared to risk everything to achieve their demands. By 1972, Freddie was also talking of the Officials as 'stickies', the name apparently given to them by the Provos as a result of what they believed were their pathetic, 'stick-in-the-mud' policies towards the Protestants and the British Government. He was even involved in physically removing some of the weapons from the Officials and transporting them to secret Provo arms caches in the Republic.

Scap was now a committed Provo and soon became a fully fledged member of the IRA, willing and happy to swear the oath of allegiance. He believed that he had found a cause he was proud to serve no matter what the consequences might be, and he readily took the three vital pledges read out to him at his initiation ceremony:

> One. No volunteer should succumb to approaches or overtures, blackmail or bribery attempts made by the enemy and should report such approaches as soon as possible.
>
> Two. Volunteers who engage in loose talk shall be dismissed.
>
> Three. Volunteers found guilty of treason face the death penalty.

Scap was sent to the Provo training camp south of the border in County Wexford, where he was given basic weapons training by Provo gunmen. He was taught to shoot proficiently with a rifle, an American MI carbine and a US-manufactured Garrard. Cool, unflustered and accurate, Scap became a crack shot and his Provo weapons instructors singled him out as a potential marksman.

Within three weeks of returning to west Belfast, Scap was recruited as a member of a Provo ASU. Now he was really put to the test, for the ASU he joined had been earmarked for special duties, ordered to carry out assassinations of British soldiers patrolling the streets of Belfast in a bid to strike terror into the hearts of the young British squaddies sent to the Province in an attempt to keep the peace. Scap remained a member of this ASU for some 12 months and he was credited by the Provos with involvement in the killings of a number of British soldiers.

Now in his 20s, and no longer such a callow youth, Scap began to realise that the Provo leadership wanted little or no involvement with the risks being taken by youngsters like him who were committed to the cause. He perceived that the leadership were never involved at the sharp end of any illegal activities; never became involved in the murderous task of actually pulling the trigger in a bid to kill a young British soldier who was simply in Belfast carrying out orders.

Scap had no personal argument with the young British soldiers patrolling the streets, and he didn't believe that killing such innocent lads, most of whom were his own age, served any useful purpose or could possibly create a situation that would lead to the British getting out of Northern Ireland and handing over power to Dublin. He also realised that it was still the Prod Loyalists, not the British Army as the Provo leadership were trying to convince him, who were barring the way to Catholics, preventing them gaining equality of rights in housing, schooling and jobs.

But, increasingly, what really bugged Scap was the attitude of the Provo leadership. He watched them at close quarters, saw the way they treated not only the young lads who were risking their necks for the cause but also the young women whom they expected to be at their beck and call. Scap would later tell his FRU handlers how he had watched senior Provos in the Republican clubs and pubs playing their roles, throwing their weight around, throwing IRA money around, buying drinks, acting the hard men and expecting to be treated like privileged leaders. And Scap knew that all the money came from collections made in bars and clubs from the hard-pressed, deprived Catholic community.

What appalled Scap's young conscience was the fact that some of those same Provo leaders also 'looked after' the young wives of some Provo members who had been arrested and imprisoned in Long Kesh. They would 'look after' them not only by providing them with financial support from IRA funds but also by becoming their lovers. Scap became so disenchanted with some Provo leaders that he would have to walk out of Republican clubs when they arrived with their mistresses. He knew that their husbands were in jail for crimes carried out on orders from those same men who were now servicing their wives.

He also saw the way the self-styled Provo leaders treated the teenage lads of west Belfast who were prepared to carry out any Provo request or order, no matter how poorly thought out or dangerous. The leaders would appeal to their youthful allegiance to the Provo cause, taking advantage of their desperation to enhance their standing within the IRA and win their spurs among their mates and their leaders. Scap knew from his own experience that many of the tasks the young lads were given bordered on the suicidal, but some of those giving such orders seemed not to care a jot that the chances of success might be only one in ten. And when such actions ended in arrest, injury or even death, those leaders would pay lip service to the bravery of the kid involved, send some money round to the grieving family, pay for his funeral and begin the search for another likely lad to carry out their orders. Scap noted that these same men hardly ever put themselves at risk.

As the months became years, Scap became more and more disillusioned, not in the fight for justice, equal rights and equal opportunities for the Catholic population but in the Provo leaders who talked of justice but, in reality, seemed merely to be revelling in their newly elevated status within the Catholic community.

The young Scap watched the trumped-up Provo leaders strutting their stuff and he noted that many seemed to take gratuitous pleasure, even a hedonistic delight, in the power they had assumed over those Catholic families they boasted they were protecting. Scap noted that it wasn't long before the protection that some of those Provo leaders were prepared to offer came with unwelcome strings – demands for money. Many Catholic businesspeople, including small shopkeepers and market traders in Belfast, Derry and other towns, were being asked to give money to the cause. At first, the small traders, shopkeepers and other firms were happy to give a donation to help those Catholic families whose husbands were imprisoned for some alleged anti-social crime, or for simply being members of the IRA. But soon the demands for money grew stronger and with the demands came menaces.

There was no gentle approach to most requests. At the first sign of protest, the warning was given, 'Pay up, or take the consequences.' If some small traders who were finding life a struggle tried to defy the Provos, they might find their shop burned out or their trade dwindling overnight as families were ordered to boycott their business. They might even find themselves taken up a dark alley and given a good beating, such was the justice of the arrogant local Provo hardmen. Scap witnessed all this going on and on several occasions he tried to appeal to the local Provos he knew as mates.

One course of action ordered by the Provo leadership seemed particularly futile and self-defeating to Scap. He could not understand why the Provos deliberately set about a systematic campaign of torching the Belfast local authority buses which served the city and its outer areas. The Belfast buses were a more vital means of transport to the Catholic community than they were to Protestant families because the Protestants had far more cars per head of the population than the Catholics. And yet, in an extraordinary, many suggested stupid and counter-productive, move, the Provos ordered their young volunteers to hijack and burn every Belfast bus they could get their hands on. Many were used as burning barricades against the RUC and the army in their street battles, but others were simply torched to rid their presence from the streets of Belfast.

There were two reasons given for this. The first, which few came to believe was true, was, the Provo leadership argued, that the Belfast buses were an affront to the Catholic minority because they were owned and run by the council, which was politically controlled by the Loyalists. The other reason suggested seemed far more likely: as a direct result of the burning of the buses, the people of Belfast were forced to use taxis.

The taxi business of Belfast, like very nearly every other part of everyday life in Northern Ireland, was run along strict religious lines. There were taxi firms that dealt exclusively with the Catholic community and another set of taxis that served the Protestants. Catholics preferring to take a taxi could jump into a black cab plying its trade along the Falls Road and pay just 10p to be dropped off anywhere along that road. With the buses gone, everyone was forced to use the taxis and the Provos then demanded £1 a day per taxi driver in protection money. As a result, the 10p fare had to be increased. Most taxis were driven by two drivers per day. It was a money-spinner that brought in some £100 a day, £700 a week, to the Provo coffers and all from the poor Catholic community. Ironically, most buses still ran in the Protestant areas so the wonderful Provo campaign to impair the Belfast Council only hit the Catholics, those same people whom the Provos were allegedly protecting and caring for.

Scap recalled to his handlers how he had witnessed the Provos telling the Catholic community that they had risen up against the hated RUC and the all-powerful Loyalists to defend the downtrodden Catholic families. Such speeches were made in church halls and in pubs and clubs by local Provo leaders. They claimed the PIRA's intention was to support them and defend their homes and families from attacks by Loyalist gangs who roamed the streets, attacking Catholic housing estates, torching Catholic houses and beating up Catholics they found straying into their territory. Scap argued that the Provos should be the successors to the great campaign for civil rights for Catholics which had exposed their lives of misery and oppression, winning them support not only from elements within the Westminster Parliament but also from the United States, where some 60 per cent of American families claimed Irish descent, though the real figure is probably nearer 15 per cent.

But the Provos, even friends of Scap's own age, didn't want to hear his protests or his pleas for a more just society within the Catholic ghettos. His vision was for a community in which the Provos collected money and distributed it among the Catholic poor, found jobs for young Catholics and used their funds to finance businesses and jobs for Catholics. They preferred to bring the battle for social justice onto the streets, draw on the money collected to buy arms, ammunition and, more importantly, bomb-making equipment which they would use to blast Belfast and the other Northern Ireland towns where Catholics lived, worked and shopped. Scap didn't see the sense in creating such mayhem, which caused the Catholic population to suffer as much as, perhaps even more than, their Protestant rivals.

And then one night in 1978, after arguments with the local Provo leadership over their treatment of an impoverished Catholic family, Scap was picked up and taken to a lonely spot where he was given a severe beating. Four Provo men, armed with sticks and batons, administered the punishment which not only left Scappaticci badly bruised but also seriously injured his pride. He was told to toe the Provo line, support the Provo cause, obey the orders handed out to him by his Provo leaders and stop his one-man campaign for social justice.

Some commentators have suggested this beating was the spur to which Scap responded by approaching the FRU and offering to work for them. But this was not the case. He never approached the authorities to offer his services as an informant. It was purely by chance that later the same year Freddie Scappaticci was stopped at an army vehicle checkpoint in Belfast and taken away for screening. Screening, as previously described, was the process initiated by British Military Intelligence. The intention was to get closer to the Catholics of Northern Ireland in the hope that they might be able to persuade some of them to work within their community for the intelligence forces in an unofficial capacity.

The success of the process relied to a great extent on the ability of the interviewers, who were selected primarily from among NCOs and senior NCOs as well as a few warrant officers, to gain the trust of those they were interviewing so that they could have further unofficial conversations with them at some future date. It was imperative for the interviewers to establish a meaningful dialogue with the man or woman being screened so that they could find some common ground and get across the point that British Military Intelligence was in Northern Ireland to help ease the situation, bring some peace and normality to the Province, protect the civil rights of the Catholic community and keep the rampaging Loyalists out of Catholic areas.

The British Army was permitted to detain the person being screened for a maximum of four hours, after which the person had either to be charged with an offence or released. In contrast, at this time the RUC was permitted to hold someone in custody for up to seven days without a charge being made.

Those army personnel who had brought Scap into the barracks for screening had not the faintest idea that he was an active Provo or that he had taken part in rioting and demonstrations, some involving violence and bloodshed, during the previous years. And, of course, they had not the slightest reason to believe that the small Italian man with a strong Belfast accent sitting in front of them had been responsible for shooting a number of British soldiers. He was simply a young Catholic who worked in a fish and chip shop. The officers had picked him up at random in the hope that he might be a suspect or might have some connection to the Provos. They hoped that four hours at the hands of an expert interviewer just might elicit some useful information for Military Intelligence.

At that meeting, of course, Scap did not tell the screening officer that he was involved with the PIRA or that he had ever been involved in rioting, targeting and shooting soldiers or RUC officers. But he did admit to supporting the Northern Ireland civil rights campaign and taking part in their demonstrations. He told them that he believed the Catholic minority were being maltreated, made to feel like second-class citizens and had suffered at the hands of the Protestants and the RUC for as long as he could remember. He also told them that he was committed to supporting the cause of civil rights for Catholics and, if necessary, would fight on behalf of his people if he was asked to do so.

Fortunately for the army, the British Government and MI5, and indirectly everyone else involved in trying to bring peace to Northern Ireland, the senior NCO responsible for initially screening Scappaticci was highly intelligent and good at his task. He never pushed Scap but simply spent some time making a connection with the young Italian.

Before walking out of the barracks, Scap agreed to meet his interviewer sometime later, but no date was fixed and he had no real intention of following it through. He had enjoyed a couple of cups of coffee and a few biscuits, and he had found the process of screening civilised and not in the least intrusive. Of course, Scap had had to provide his name, address and occupation, and to give details of his next of kin. It was very useful for him, while he was hiding his membership of the IRA, that he had an occupation, working in the family fish and chip shop, for the great majority of those young 20-somethings picked up for screening had no jobs, very little formal education and were pinpointed as prime targets for the Provo recruitment teams.

Though no suggestion was made at that first interview that the army would want him to act as an informer or a go-between, Scap suspected a trap. He was no ordinary Catholic lad with little ambition, little education and no plans for his future. Scap could not and did not believe that his army contact merely wanted to see him with a view to helping the Catholic cause.

Despite his suspicions, however, within the next three months Scap had returned on three occasions for coffee, biscuits and a chat with his interviewer, and the two had struck up a relationship. They would talk in private for an hour or more. At first, Scap was not keen to talk, to discuss anything at all, for he still believed the army were planning to use him for some plan or other. One of the reasons he kept returning was that he wanted to find out why the NCO was so keen to keep the relationship going. He was intrigued but convinced that the NCO had no idea that he was a Provo or that he had taken the oath of allegiance to the IRA. He simply could not understand why the British Army had become so interested in him.

And then, almost imperceptibly, Scap realised that he had begun to look forward to his friendly chats over a cup of coffee, and he started to feel that the NCO shared his views of the unfair way the Catholic minority had been treated by the Protestant majority over many, many years. On occasions, during conversations with his interviewer, Scap would ask whether Catholics would one day be granted all their civil rights. He also asked whether the NCO believed the British Army would remain in Northern Ireland for good as a bulwark of law and order between the Protestants and the Catholics. Scap found that the more they talked, the more they had in common, sharing the same beliefs in freedom and justice for all, and a fair crack of the whip for everyone in Northern Ireland. Within those first three months he had built up a close association with his NCO and yet his handler had never even asked if he was a member of the Provisional IRA or had ever taken part in any illegal demonstrations, marches or riots, ever taken up arms against the British Army, ever used a handgun or a rifle or ever thrown petrol bombs at the RUC or the British Army – none of the questions that Scap had anticipated being asked. Already, in his open-handed discussions with his handler, Scap had come to accept that the British Army were only doing the bloody impossible job of trying to keep the peace.

The Royal Ulster Constabulary remained a different matter. Like nearly every other Catholic in Northern Ireland, Scap did not trust the RUC one jot. He believed they were simply a bunch of hardline Loyalists in police uniform who were readily prepared to carry out the dirty work of the Protestant majority. Scap had also hated the infamous B Specials, the reserve police force of Northern Ireland brought in to deal with demonstrations and illegal marches when the RUC felt overwhelmed by the number of protestors. The B Specials were seen by Catholics as the rough, tough element of not only the RUC but also the Loyalist factions within the Protestant community.

He knew that the B Specials were quite prepared to batter the Catholics into submission using as much violence as they felt was needed to restore order. And indeed, it would appear that many B Specials did see their voluntary work within the RUC as an opportunity to vent their spleen, their prejudices, their anger and their hatred towards the Catholics in the violence they were permitted to use against them whenever they were called out. Many Loyalists appeared to enjoy the opportunity to batter defenceless Catholics, break a few heads, rout the Catholic demonstrators and restore what they had come to believe was the official status quo: Protestants in command, Catholics in submission. Nothing his handler could say would change Scap's opinion of these men.

As the meetings continued, Scap gradually became aware that he was being asked, very subtly, to provide scraps of information, for example about favourite Republican clubs or pubs and whether anyone he knew frequented them on a regular basis. He came to realise that in doing so he might in fact be playing a part in an effort to stop the rioting and internecine warfare on the streets. During these early months, even when he provided the odd piece of information, the matter of money was never raised and Scap did not ask for any. Of course, his friendly NCO now knew that Scap's parents owned a fish and chip shop and that he worked there earning a reasonable wage. Usually, odd titbits of information from youngsters picked up in the screening process were rewarded with a few quid, the recipient quickly understanding that the more information he provided, the more money he would earn. Word naturally got around and some young teenage Catholic lads would sometimes provide information, any information, as long as it earned them a few pounds. For many, the money became the incentive to tell stories.

A few months after his first visit to the Military Intelligence offices, after he had finally revealed that he was in fact a member of the Provisional IRA, Scap had a long heart-to-heart with his NCO handler in which, for the first time, he criticised the Provo leadership, accusing them of simply using the Catholic community and their demands for civil rights as a cover for their real campaign: a campaign of violence which they planned to unleash against the Protestants, the RUC and the British Army in a bid to convince the British Government that the only way to ensure peace in Northern Ireland was to do a deal with the Government of the Republic of Ireland. Encouraged by his interviewer, Scap took that opportunity to unburden all his grievances with the Provo leadership, explaining in detail some of their more outrageous bully-boy behaviour.

At this early stage – the late 1970s – the IRA apparently had no intention of unleashing what would later become an indiscriminate bombing campaign on mainland Britain with the intention of killing and maiming as many ordinary British men, women and children as possible. According to Scappaticci, the IRA's initial bombing campaigns were aimed at destabilising ordinary life in Northern

Ireland in the hope of forcing the British Government into a deal.

This information from the heart of the Provisional IRA was of paramount importance not only to British Military Intelligence but also to MI5 and the British Government in London. However, Scap's identity, even his existence, was not leaked to the Northern Ireland political leadership or Northern Ireland's senior civil servants, the RUC, the RUC Special Branch or senior Ulster Unionist politicians. Only those few MI5 and British Military Intelligence handlers and their senior officers knew of Scap's existence, and even then his importance was forever being played down. Almost overnight, Scap had unknowingly become a crucial cog at the heart of British Intelligence within Northern Ireland. This was just the beginning, but Freddie Scappaticci would become the most important undercover agent in the history of Northern Ireland.

To maintain the secrecy surrounding their top agent's identity, a set of rooms was built below ground in one of the headquarter buildings which housed the Force Research Unit, that part of Military Intelligence who 'ran' Steak Knife. Only a restricted number of senior NCOs, warrant officers and senior officers were ever permitted entry, and the room was not only guarded on a permanent 24-hour basis but also continually manned. The air-conditioned subterranean room was nicknamed the 'Rat Hole'.

For much of the time, Scap's meetings with his handlers followed the same pattern as most agents': a phone call, a pick-up in a car watched by two other vehicles manned by armed officers and then a drive to a secret safe house somewhere in Belfast. The drop-off would be conducted in the same way. On several occasions, however, Scap would visit the Rat Hole, though he was never seen arriving or departing. Most FRU officers had no idea that the Rat Hole had been constructed solely for Steak Knife's sake, believing it was just a top-secret location, totally secure from potential electronic eavesdropping and a place where senior officers could chat away in the knowledge that it was the one really secure place in the whole of Belfast.

Scap's handler suggested that he should consider taking a more senior role in the IRA so that one day he might have some control over those Provos whom he despised for their attitudes to the Catholic population, notably the young enthusiastic kids, the wives of those in jail and particularly the small traders from whom they were extorting money. Having taken this advice, Scap volunteered to become a member of the IRA's infamous interrogation and punishment squad, the notorious 'Nutting Squad', responsible for internal security within the Provisional IRA as well as for questioning Provo members suspected of passing information to the RUC Special Branch, British Military Intelligence or MI5.

Such interrogations often took place in the Republic, where the Provos believed they would be able to proceed without interruption. Scap would be asked to travel down from the North to cross-question suspects, if necessary to the point of death. From these interviews, Scap would be privy to secret information that could be of use to the intelligence services. Playing the interrogator and torturer at the very heart of the IRA was, of course, also the perfect cover for an undercover agent working for the British.

The information Scap gleaned from such interrogations varied widely from chit-chat nonsense to important contacts and even, on occasions, forthcoming IRA bombing plans. Scap was able to provide the names of those he was told to interrogate, give the reasons for those interrogations, give the names of senior Provos ordering the interrogations and, of course, sometimes discover from the person he was interrogating and torturing the names or codenames of handlers, their methods of recruitment, their meeting places and detailed descriptions of their appearance. Armed with this information, he was able to warn the FRU when their handlers had been placed at risk.

Every member of the IRA knew that supplying information to the enemy was always, but always, punishable by death. There were no second chances. As a result, of course, nobody was going to admit to an act of treason easily. Those involved in interrogating such suspects therefore had to apply awesome pressure to make the suspects confess. Scap became very adept not only at interrogation but also in his methods of torture, which he would apply when suspects resisted questioning or were suspected of lying. In fact, within a matter of six months, Scap had built a fearsome reputation for himself within the Provisional leadership as the PIRA's most clinical, ruthless and successful interrogator. If a suspect survived his torture techniques, the Provo leadership believed they must be innocent because Scap would drive people almost to the point of death time after time in a bid to extract the truth from them.

But Scap was not responsible for the assassination of the traitors. When a man or woman had finally confessed, there were no further questions asked. Scap would walk away from the scene and one of the senior Provos present would order the suspect to be taken to a deserted spot, often outside Belfast, where they would be forced to their knees, hands tied behind their back and unceremoniously shot in the back of the head, usually with a single bullet. The bodies were never buried but deliberately left in the open so that they would be easily discovered and the victim's fate revealed to one and all as a warning to others never to betray the cause.

Scap's unique position within the IRA allowed him to move easily through the ranks to become one of the most reliable and trusted adjuncts of the Provo leadership, accepted not only by those Provo leaders in the Belfast Brigade of the IRA but also by members of the IRA's Army Council, who decided policies and were responsible for directing the general thrust of the war on the ground. For example, the Army Council would decide whether they believed the political climate in Britain was now right for them to change the emphasis of their attacks and bomb the British mainland, and they would also select the targets, whether pubs or shopping areas, the City of London or army establishments.

The Provo leadership had every reason to trust Scap and, over time, they did so implicitly. His short biography was impeccable. He had manned the barricades with them in the early days and fought street battles against the hated B Specials and the RUC, and later the British Army. Scap had become an invisible, unknown thorn in the side of the security services, a crack shot who could keep a dozen police officers or even soldiers hiding behind cover for fear the invisible marksman would kill them the moment they broke cover.

One such incident took place during rioting in the Falls Road in the late 1970s when young Provo demonstrators hijacked two buses and torched them, creating a blazing barrier across the road. When the RUC and the army arrived on the scene, in which some 300 young men were taking part – hurling petrol bombs, stones and bricks, and using powerful catapults – the RUC quickly realised that a Provo marksman was also at work on the other side of the blazing buses. Every time the fire brigade approached in an attempt to put out the raging fires, shots were being fired. These shots weren't aimed directly at the firemen or the RUC officers, but they were left in little doubt that the marksman was giving warning that if they encroached further then they might get shot. On that occasion, Scap kept the forces of law and order at bay for more than an hour while the young Provo teenagers used the buses as protection against the RUC and their rubber bullets. His constant peppering of the area also made it impossible for the army to send in snatch squads to pick up the ringleaders and take them away. The security forces realised that the Provo gunman had to be a remarkable marksman because his shots were so accurate, so very different from the usual volley of random gunfire the RUC and the army would face in such situations. This unidentified marksman would fire only a few accurate shots and then move position so that it was all but impossible for the army marksmen to keep track of his movements. Such shooting won much praise from the Provo leadership and, as a result, Scap became a hero of the barricades.

He had also taken the pledge to become a full member of the IRA and had proved himself a young man who would lay his life on the line for the cause of a united Ireland. By his dedication to the cause, by his involvement in street fighting, by his treatment of suspected traitors, Scap became accepted as one of the IRA's most important men, on a par with the leadership, though not totally accepted as one of the Provo leaders because, of course, he was not of Irish blood.

Some Provo leaders always wondered why Scap, an Italian, should want to become so involved in the cause of a united Ireland, prepared to risk his life or certainly his freedom in the same way as every other IRA member. Some wondered why he was fighting their battle for equality. Scap would explain that he had become involved because he had been brought up from childhood mixing with young Catholics of his own age, living the same life as they did, treated as a lower-class person by the Protestant majority. He had fought for the civil rights campaign because he truly believed that everyone should enjoy the same rights and have equal opportunities. These views of his never changed, not even when he began working for British Military Intelligence.

To the Force Research Unit, and later MI5, Scap rapidly became the most important agent that ever worked for the Brits throughout the last three decades of the century. Scap knew almost everything about the Provisional IRA, their plans, their targets, their bombing campaigns and some of their arms dumps. He also reported to his handlers the internal squabbles of the Provo leadership, the thinking of the various factions, and he would report whose star was rising and whose was falling. This was, of course, tremendously important to the boffins of MI5, who were always attempting to second-guess in what direction the Provo leadership was moving.

Indeed, it was to be Scappaticci's reports to MI5 in the 1990s that revealed for the first time that there were certain members of the Army Council who believed their 30-year uprising had reached a stalemate and perhaps the time had come to bring an end to the violence and bombings; that efforts should be made to try and achieve the same objectives by political bargaining. They knew that successive British governments were desperate to bring the Troubles to an end and they believed British voters had become so fed up with Northern Ireland that they simply wanted an end to what had become a bloody nuisance. The British Army had also become fed up with the lack of political progress in Northern Ireland because recruiting sergeants had come to discover by the early 1990s that young men were not interested in joining the army simply because they had no wish to risk their lives patrolling the dangerous streets of Northern Ireland.

The esteem in which Scap was held by the security services and British Government is illustrated by the interest taken in him by those in the highest echelons of power. When the Prime Minister at the time, Margaret Thatcher, had been briefed by the head of MI5 about their prize agent, she insisted on seeing every piece of information he was passing through to his handlers in the Force Research Unit, from whom MI5 were receiving their briefings.

Before Scap arrived on the scene, the quality of intelligence from the Catholic community and, of course, the Provos was pathetic and, for months and sometimes years at a time, almost non-existent. There was a void of ignorance concerning the thinking and overall planning of the IRA's Army Council – the movement's policy makers – and senior MI5 officers would be tasked with outlining what they believed or understood to be the latest tactics and plans of the Provo leadership – a thankless and near-impossible job.

Almost alone, Scappaticci succeeded in filling that void. And Mrs Thatcher gave so much credence to his views, his ideas, his reports to his FRU handlers that she would ask for the FRU officers' reports – Military Intelligence Source Reports (MISRs) – to be forwarded directly to her in their entirety. Usually in such circumstances, a cabinet minister would simply ask for a précis of those MISRs to be forwarded to them so that they could get a flavour of what was happening on the ground. Mrs Thatcher, however, insisted on seeing every word, every jot and tittle of Scap's reports. On numerous occasions she would also demand to debrief Scap's handlers, wanting to know everything about the Italian fish and chip shop worker who, virtually on his own, was responsible for providing British Military Intelligence, MI5 and senior politicians and analysts with the information they needed in the struggle to counter the activities of the Provisional IRA.

At weekly meetings of the Government's Joint Intelligence Committee, which Mrs Thatcher frequently chaired at No. 10 Downing Street, she would ask the head of MI5 to read out extracts from the MISRs that had come from Scap. She let those members of the top brass who attended such gatherings know that they should pay great attention to every scrap of information supplied by Scappaticci because she rated him so highly. On one occasion, Mrs Thatcher impressed on the committee members that they must do everything in their power to protect Scappaticci because he was the most important person working for the British in Northern Ireland. Everyone round the table nodded in agreement. This piece of information was made known to this author's contacts and passed on for the purposes of this book.

Thatcher's belief in Steak Knife's trusted reports led to her inviting Scap to Chequers in 1986 to spend a long weekend with her and to meet other members of the Joint Intelligence Committee to discuss the current thinking within the Provo leadership. Later, Scap would report back to his handlers that he was taken aback by the treatment he was given at Chequers. He was told by Mrs Thatcher to ask for anything he wanted and he would be given it; to do anything he wanted and permission would be granted; to ask any questions and, importantly, to join in all their discussions and to bring up any matter he wished, no matter how trivial.

At their discussions, Mrs Thatcher would constantly ask Scap for his views on any points being raised because, as she explained to him, he was the only person around the table who really knew the people they were discussing and how they were thinking. It was also in a private fireside chat with Mrs Thatcher that she told him that he must permit the British Government to make secret but substantial regular payments into a bank account which would be opened discreetly for him and which he would be the only person with access to. Embarrassed by the question of money, Scap had no idea what was being offered and he suggested that Mrs Thatcher should suggest a figure. She suggested that the Government should pay him £75,000 a year which would be tax-free. Mrs Thatcher added that the payments would be backdated to when he began working for the Force Research Unit. They shook hands. Scap was somewhat taken aback but readily accepted the offer. He knew that, if anything ever happened to him, the money would go to his wife and children. The account was opened by MI5 in a British bank based in Gibraltar.

Back on the ground, Scap continued his remarkable double life, a life in which he continued to supply vital information to his FRU handlers but which also on occasion involved him carrying out the most ghastly interrogation and torture of mainly young men and a few women who had been persuaded, usually by money, to work for the RUC Special Branch, the FRU or, very infrequently, MI5.

Many people, including this author, face a dilemma when examining the contradictory life and career of Freddie Scappaticci. On the one hand, he was the most important undercover agent working for the British Government throughout 25 years of the Troubles and the intelligence he provided not only thwarted many PIRA bombings and shootings, saving the lives of unknown numbers of potential victims, but also saved the lives of a number of individuals specifically targeted by the Provos.

On the other hand, of course, he personally carried out the most despicable and horrendous torture of a number of Provos who had betrayed the IRA cause. From time to time, almost as if he was seeking absolution, Scap would be compelled to discuss this part of his undercover work with his handlers because he found perpetrating such acts against another human being abhorrent, especially when the person confessed. Even as he conducted his interrogation, Scappaticci knew then that the person he was terrorising could be dead within hours, if not minutes, and all as a result of his ferocious treatment, which sometimes involved the most gruesome and blood-curdling forms of torture imaginable.

During one meeting in the late 1980s, Scap explained to his handlers how he was able to continue interrogating and torturing people, strangers he had never known and usually never met. He explained that he saw those traitors as corrupt, because for the most part they were selling their information for cash: information that would often lead to the arrest or killing of their own comrades. Scappaticci also explained to his handlers that the way he justified his own behaviour was that he believed the only way forward for the intractable Northern Ireland sectarian problem was dialogue, not bombings and shootings which killed so many innocent people and brought terror and misery to the innocent citizens of Belfast and Northern Ireland. He hoped that the intelligence he was gathering and passing on would help to hasten the end of the conflict on the streets.

Those handlers who knew Scap well contend that he was no sadist, not an evil man or a monster who enjoyed his horrible work. He was a realist who knew that to hold the position which enabled him to save lives and prevent bombings he needed to be feared by one and all throughout the Provo army of volunteers, from the highest to the lowest. In that way, Scap realised he had built up a formidable protective screen for himself that no one dared challenge for fear that one day he might be interrogating them. And Scappaticci was perfectly at peace in his mind about betraying the IRA cause because he believed that the PIRA was rotten to the core. He considered that the ideals and ambitions of the civil rights campaign which he had readily espoused and fought for had been hijacked by the Provo leadership, who were prepared to sacrifice as many lives as they deemed necessary to achieve their ambition of uniting the Six Counties with the Republic. And in the process the Provo leadership continued to reap the financial rewards. He knew that Provo leaders had steadily accrued for themselves expensive houses and very healthy bank accounts, while they urged the new young recruits to give all, including their lives if necessary, for the cause. When the leadership realised in the late 1980s that their ambitions were obviously beyond their capabilities, they set about seeking a political solution through which they hoped to enjoy continued wealth, status and respected positions within a Northern Ireland government.

It is not known how many such interrogations were carried out by Scap, or how many people he tortured. Nor has this author been able to ascertain precisely how many alleged PIRA traitors or informers were shot dead as a direct result of Scappaticci's interrogations, but an informed guesstimate by his handlers put the number at less than 50, still a shocking number.

Scappaticci only talked to his handlers about those Provos and others he interrogated and tortured if he discovered intelligence which he believed his handlers should be made aware of. Indeed, in his chats with handlers, Scap never mentioned the actual torture techniques he employed to extract information. It was not something of which he was proud. His handlers would have seen the police and coroner's reports on the bodies of the executed 'traitors' and in that way they learned of the ferocity of Scap's work. They did not question him about his methods, as they believed that was a matter for Scappaticci and his own conscience. Intelligence officers who have talked to this author, however, are convinced that it was necessary for Scap to continue his role of interrogator-in-chief for the Provos because it gave him the most extraordinary cover for his real role as the eyes and ears of the British Government in Northern Ireland.

But there was another vital reason why MI5 wanted Scap to continue his dastardly role as torturer-in-chief and that was the fact that, on a few occasions, Scap was able to organise the rescue of undercover British agents and touts whom the IRA suspected of betraying the cause.

Chapter Four

MASTER SPY, TORTURER, PIMPERNEL

One of Freddie Scappaticci's most dramatic rescues in the late 1980s involved a talented young FRU agent named Jimmy, who had been working undercover for the Force Research Unit in south Armagh, mixing with the hardline Provos who controlled the vast majority of that county. Many people in mainland Britain find it difficult to comprehend that south Armagh – a part of the United Kingdom – was to all intents and purposes a no-go area not only to ordinary Brits but also to the British Army and the RUC. That, however, was the reality.

An indication of the danger faced by British forces who manned the base near the border was the fact that when RAF helicopters ferried people and cargo to the base with ammunition and vital supplies, troops had to be deployed for hundreds of yards around the base to provide the protection necessary to ensure Provo gunmen did not get near enough to hit the choppers as they landed and took off from the base. During times of high tension in Northern Ireland, the south Armagh base was often hit daily by incoming mortar bombs fired from only a hundred yards or so beyond the perimeter fence. Indeed, those troops who spent any length of time at the south Armagh army base felt they were living in a permanent state of siege and, understandably, they resented the fact.

And that was why the courage of Jimmy was admired by everyone in the Force Research Unit, who realised the extraordinary risks he was taking on a daily basis, living and operating in that area of Northern Ireland.

One of Jimmy's claims to fame was that he had provided the information which led directly to the security forces unearthing a Provo bomb factory which contained 1,000 lb of explosives and two 'ringed' vehicles: a truck and a saloon car. A 'ringed' vehicle was one identical in make, colour, engine capacity, number plate and general condition to another vehicle owned and run by an ordinary person who would have no idea the Provos had an identical vehicle at their disposal. These ringed vehicles were used by the Provos as a cover, so that when RUC officers or soldiers at vehicle checkpoints (VCPs) checked the details, the vehicle would flash up on their screens as being legitimately owned by a member of the public who was above suspicion.

These two ringed vehicles had been used from time to time by the Provos to carry out bombing missions: the truck to transport the explosives, the car for the getaway. On this occasion the bomb was to be planted near Dundalk in County Monaghan allegedly on orders from the infamous Thomas 'Slab' Murphy, one-time officer commanding the Provos' Northern Command. The target was apparently a police station in or near Newry. On this occasion, the bombing was thwarted thanks to Agent Jimmy, but some time later Newry police station was subjected to a heavy mortar attack which killed several people.

On another occasion Jimmy informed his FRU handlers that a different south Armagh Provo team was planning to destroy a bridge on the main Belfast to Dublin railway line, timed to explode as a passenger train was passing overhead. The plan was to blow up the bridge, which would possibly also blow up the train, killing or injuring scores of passengers. The Provos knew that blowing the bridge would bring the army and the RUC to the scene to help in the rescue and to guard the passengers, the fire and ambulance crews as they took away the injured. The Provos then planned to launch their mortar and small arms attack to cause the maximum casualties and maximum mayhem. This operation was also successfully thwarted, thanks to Jimmy.

Agent Jimmy was close to both the Provos and to the INLA. This was a very rare position, as the two terrorist organisations were ideologically opposed to each other and argued vehemently over the different ways each wanted to prosecute the war against the Loyalists and the British Government. As a result of trying to straddle the two terror groups, Jimmy found himself coming under suspicion from both of them, not because either considered he might be a British agent but because the two organisations were so deeply suspicious of each other they didn't like anyone having contacts in the rival group.

As was often the case, Jimmy was enjoying a quiet lunchtime drink in The Stag's Head in Dundalk, minding his own business, when two of his accomplices from the INLA entered the bar and walked over to him.

In a whisper, one said, 'You're coming for a ride with us, Jimmy. Someone wants to talk to you. Don't try anything, we're armed.'

Jimmy had no option but to go with his colleagues. He feared the worst. He was ordered into the back of a waiting car outside the pub. There were two INLA thugs in the front and two others climbed in either side of him to prevent any possible escape. Jimmy would later tell his handler, 'My heart was thumping from the moment my mate told me someone wanted to talk to me. As we walked out of the pub I just kept saying over and over, "shit, shit, shit". And when I was surrounded by four of them in that car I was convinced my days were numbered. I just kept telling myself that the only way of escaping from this alive was to keep my head and keep cool. In my mind I was fairly certain the INLA had nothing on me because I had been so very, very careful and I wondered what on earth they had discovered to treat me as an informer.

'We drove south out of Dundalk and a blindfold was placed around my head. My so-called mate kept telling me that there was nothing to worry about but that they were only obeying orders from the leadership. They had been told to pick me up and bring me back for questioning. Allegedly, he had no idea why they had ordered me to be brought in blindfold.'

Later he would recount in great detail to his handler exactly what happened. 'After about 30 minutes the car stopped and the blindfold was taken off. We were in a farmyard but I had no idea exactly where we were. I had tried to figure out the route as we drove south, but I did that to keep me mentally alert as much as anything else. In reality, I had no idea where we were.

'As my eyes became accustomed to the daylight, I looked around and saw three blokes with guns standing around the farmyard. It was obvious that they had been expecting me, for the guns were pointing at me. We all walked into the kitchen and I immediately noticed two UZI machine guns lying on the table in the centre of the room. The magazines were in the guns but I couldn't tell whether there were any rounds in the mags. But I knew the UZIs were only academic because there was no way I was going to get out of that place unless I managed to convince them that I was not guilty of whatever they had on me.'

Standing in the kitchen was the INLA leader, the infamous, fanatical Dominic 'Mad Dog' McGlinchey. McGlinchey, a well-built man aged around 30, had dedicated his life to violence, terrorism, the overthrow of the Ulster Unionist Government and kicking the British out of Northern Ireland. His wife Mary was also present. They were drinking tea and appeared casual and unruffled. Jimmy was ordered to take everything out of his pockets and place the contents on the table. All he had in his pockets were his car keys and a few pounds. He was then searched but nothing else was discovered.

'Sit over there,' Mad Dog told him.

The moment Jimmy had seen Mad Dog standing in the kitchen he had become seriously worried because he knew of his reputation as a ruthless killer who didn't seem to give a damn who he killed or why. He just seemed to enjoy the power he got from it. There were some who believed Mad Dog was the ultimate killer, someone who really did get kicks from murdering people.

'Where?' Jimmy asked, looking around him.

'On top of the cooker,' Mad Dog said menacingly, pointing to the gas cooker standing against the wall. Jimmy wondered if this was the start of the torture and he feared Mad Dog would light the gas hobs if he didn't provide the answers he wanted. Jimmy felt a lump in his throat and his heart beat faster, but he kept telling himself to stay cool.

Three of the men who had travelled down to the farmhouse in the car were standing around the kitchen, guns in their hands. Two put down their weapons, grabbed Jimmy by his arms and lifted him onto the cooker. The questions began, coming thick and fast, but Jimmy was relieved that Mad Dog made no move to turn on the gas hobs. Jimmy believed that, 'Mad Dog realised that the gas hobs were more of a menace to me if he did not turn them on. [He believed] that I would tell the truth for fear that if I told lies he would simply switch on the gas hobs and light them.'

Mad Dog continued the interrogation for 30 minutes, but throughout he was polite, speaking quietly, never raising his voice or threatening Jimmy with any repercussions. For his part, Jimmy was able to answer each and every question thrown at him, as most of them involved his relationship with the Provisional IRA. Indeed, by the end of 30 minutes Mad Dog had not even mentioned British Intelligence, let alone asked any specific questions about the forces of law and order. Jimmy could hardly believe his ears when Mad Dog turned to the others and said, 'I'm happy.'

He then turned to Jimmy and said, 'You've answered all the questions. I'm going to get you driven back to Dundalk or wherever you want to be dropped.' He then put his hand in his pocket, took out a few notes and stuffed them in Jimmy's shirt pocket, saying, 'Here's some money to have a drink.'

Jimmy was taken off the cooker and two men walked either side of him out of the kitchen to the car waiting in the farmyard outside. Once again two men sat in the front while two others sat either side of him in the back. Once again he was blindfolded. Jimmy felt certain that Mad Dog's final words were a sham and that he was about to be executed. The longer the car ride, however, the more Jimmy's hopes were raised that he might indeed be heading back to Dundalk and the safety of his home. But he didn't let himself get carried away with elation because he knew that at any moment the car might come to a stop and he might be facing a bullet.

About 30 minutes later, the car did come to a halt and the hood over his head was taken off. He realised he was in a town and suddenly recognised that he was in fact on the outskirts of Dundalk. Finally he began to believe that he was safe. The car drove to The Stag's Head and stopped. He was told to get out and go and have a drink.

He would tell his handler, 'As I walked into the pub, I felt as though I had lived my entire life in those last few hours. I was full of joy, elated beyond belief and so very, very relieved I could hardly contain myself. I put my hand in my shirt pocket and found Mad Dog had handed over forty punts. I had one drink, the most wonderful glass of Guinness I had ever drunk in my life. And then I went home, straight home.'

On another occasion some months later, Jimmy was invited to meet some Provo colleagues in The Sportsman's Bar on the main Newry to Dublin road. Before they even offered Jimmy a drink, one of the men said, 'We need to go in the back for a chat,' a normal enough precaution when the Provos needed to discuss their private affairs.

When Jimmy walked into the room, however, he found four armed blokes standing around the room and a big fat Irish woman in her 30s standing facing him. She seemed to be in command. She began by inviting Jimmy to take a seat on a chair that had been placed in the centre of the room. The second he sat down, the woman nodded to two of the men, who came forward and tied him to the chair, his arms trussed behind it so he couldn't move. Without saying a word, the woman walked up to him and gave him a resounding smack across the face. Then she gave him a few more hard smacks as though to soften him up. Throughout this, she said not a word, but the look on her face was one of loathing and disgust.

Once again Jimmy feared the worst; once again he searched his memory, wondering if he had let anything slip, made any silly mistake which had alerted the Provos to the fact that he might be a British agent. After a few more slaps, the woman then stood back and began asking him questions. And to Jimmy's great relief the questions this time centred on his relationship with the INLA. The fat woman wanted to know whether he knew anything about a shooting by INLA activists who had somehow captured two Provo gunmen, put them in the boot of a car and then killed them with a shotgun. The woman had been led to believe that Jimmy might have been involved, but he was able to provide sound evidence proving that he was nowhere near the place at the time.

Jimmy's problem was that he was one of those young men who was friendly with everyone. He was on first-name terms with most of the INLA and Provo activists who lived in south Armagh and towns further north. He stopped to talk with them, drank in bars with them, treated them all as his mates. Jimmy would always volunteer to run errands for either organisation because, once again, that gave him more knowledge and more access to the local leaders. It also helped him in his real task of working as an undercover British agent, and that was the principal reason he continued to see both sets of young men and treat them as his friends. Jimmy was one of those agents working for the British for one reason – money. In fact, he didn't earn a good living from Military Intelligence, usually a few hundred pounds a month. But he was one of that rare breed of young men who also enjoyed the danger, knowing that if he was caught his life would be snuffed out by a bullet in the back of the head.

Over a drink, Jimmy would frequently persuade an INLA man to give him some information about the Provos and vice versa, and he would then pass both those pieces of information on to his FRU handlers. Indeed, Jimmy would say later that most of the first-class intelligence he was able to provide to his handlers on the two terror organisations came from the rival group.

Jimmy was recognised by both organisations as a small-time criminal who eked out a living smuggling cigarettes and hard liquor into Northern Ireland and selling them through a regular circle of mates he met in pubs and clubs. He was also known to dabble in stolen goods, but mostly around Christmas-time when people wanted to buy presents on the cheap.

He hadn't really taken offence at the bullying tactics of the Provo woman, who seemed to like acting tough, because he knew he was on safe territory. Not once did she ask any questions about the British or even suggest that he might be involved with any British undercover operation. After 20 minutes of a stream of questions that he found easy to answer, the woman stepped back and said in a commanding voice, 'I'm finished.'

She then told Jimmy to remain in the room with his two mates for ten minutes until her team had left, and then he was to go next door and have a drink. After that, he was free to go home. Jimmy recalled later, 'Once again, I really enjoyed that pint of Guinness safe in the knowledge that my two mates had not the faintest idea why I appeared so relaxed and at ease with the world.'

But Jimmy's luck was about to run out.

A raw, inexperienced 17-year-old clerk had just been employed as the tea boy and office junior at Bessbrook Mill, one of the FRU's main centres of operation. It was the teenager's first posting. In every FRU office there were always two separate black plastic bags for rubbish: one for non-sensitive material, old envelopes, etc., and a second black plastic bag clearly marked 'For Burning Only'. These bags contained sensitive and sometimes top-secret material which, if it fell into the hands of the Provos, could result in undercover agents being exposed and perhaps tortured and murdered. The bags marked 'For Burning Only' were taken directly from the office each day by FRU personnel and burned in an incinerator on site. There was no way such material could then fall into enemy hands.

On this particular evening, the young lad was tidying up and, by mistake, placed a 'For Burning Only' plastic bag on the skip which was taken away by the local binmen once a week to the nearby Newry tip. As luck would have it, the binmen collected the skip from the FRU offices the very next morning. There was usually nothing in the black bags that would be of the slightest interest to the Provos or anyone else, but on this occasion, as the binman emptied his skip onto the tip, he noticed the black bag with the large yellow lettering 'For Burning Only'. He was fairly certain the bag must have come from the British base at Bessbrook Mill and decided to have a look inside. He realised almost immediately that what he found in the bag would be of real importance to the Provisional IRA, with whom his sympathies lay. He took the bag and went round to see one of his Provo mates.

One quick examination of the contents told the Provo activist that his local commander would find the contents extremely useful. Handed the plastic bag, the local Provo commanders could hardly believe their luck when they tipped out its entire contents and examined each and every piece of paper. Inside the bag there were the records of a long and detailed meeting between FRU handlers and Agent Jimmy. The records, all immaculately typed, were a treasure trove of top-secret information revealing the names and ranks of the handlers operating within Bessbrook Mill; the registration numbers and types of cars used by handlers; the pick-up and drop-off points for FRU touts and agents; the length of meetings; and, most important of all, details of every piece of intelligence that Jimmy had given his FRU handler that day.

Jimmy's name was not revealed in any of the records, only his number had been written down, and as a result Dundalk PIRA could not at first identify the source. The local PIRA chiefs were called together for an urgent meeting and were all shown the small mountain of paper that had been found in the plastic bag. However, it took them a couple of days to come to the conclusion that the evidence before them showed that the most likely suspect was young Jimmy. And they still weren't 100 per cent certain. On the Tuesday following the discovery, and still unsure whether Jimmy was their man, it was decided to send two armed men to his home, pick him up and bring him in for questioning.

The Provos realised they needed to work quickly because they had to assume that as soon as the Force Research Unit discovered that a bag had gone missing they would immediately mount an operation to ensure the safety of anyone they believed might be compromised. But on the Monday morning, the Force Research Unit staff were unaware that the highly sensitive plastic bag had gone missing.

Then two events changed everything. On the Monday, Steak Knife received a message from his Provo chief of staff that he was to go south immediately to interrogate a suspected FRU agent whom the Dundalk PIRA leaders had unearthed but not yet arrested. Scap left his home in Belfast and travelled to the deserted farmhouse south of the border where he had been told the suspect would be taken. When he arrived, he was briefed by another Provo interrogator that the suspect's name might be Jimmy and that they were almost certain he was an undercover agent working for British Military Intelligence.

Steak Knife was briefed that the Provo leadership believed this suspect could potentially be of enormous importance. Because of their suspicions, he had been told to give the suspect the full treatment, using whatever means necessary to ensure that he revealed every scrap of intelligence about the organisation he worked for, his handlers, his contacts within the community and the names of any other spies he had been working with. Only after ascertaining the spy had been 'squeezed dry' should Scap hand him over for execution.

This unusual message from the Provo leadership convinced Steak Knife that the Provos must have captured someone of real significance to the Force Research Unit. The black plastic bag had been removed from Bessbrook Mill, which, of course, he knew to be one of the FRU's top-secret administrative centres. Through his usual channels, Scap immediately contacted his FRU agent and told him what was happening, and, more to the point, the details of how the source had been discovered.

This put the FRU in an immediate state of full alert, some suggested near-panic. This was the worst possible news that any government agency running undercover agents could receive. Indeed, agents working in that FRU office at that time suggested the news sent shockwaves through the organisation, for they realised the full implications of what had occurred and what the probable consequences would be for Jimmy.

The alarming news was passed to MI5 headquarters in London and senior government officials in Belfast. All FRU handlers were ordered to report immediately to their respective offices and document security staff were ordered to Bessbrook to investigate the procedural flaws behind this serious breach of security.

Jimmy's FRU handlers did not know the identities of all his contacts. But they feared that if Jimmy was given the full ghastly torture treatment there was a real probability that the FRU would face a meltdown of their entire network of agents in south Armagh, a network which had taken years of patient endeavour to build. During the previous 12 months in particular, and thanks mainly to Jimmy, the Force Research Unit was finally receiving first-class intelligence from south Armagh and they had managed to piece together valuable information about both the Provos' and the INLA's activities, their arms dumps, their meeting places, their hierarchy and their training grounds.

At an urgent meeting of senior FRU staff and Jimmy's personal handlers the decision was taken, with the full agreement of the TCG, that everything possible must be done to rescue him before the IRA were able to come to the conclusion that Jimmy was indeed the FRU agent. Steak Knife had told his handlers that he had been sent south to question someone the Provos believed to be a FRU agent but that the man had not yet been picked up. Scap informed them that the agent was likely to be 'arrested' by the Provos within the next 12 hours, if not sooner.

Through the usual channels of communication, a message was sent to Jimmy, telling him to 'Come North Immediately'. His handlers knew that Jimmy would know the place to report to, but to their astonishment and consternation FRU handlers received a reply saying, 'Can't attend. Too much on. Re-arrange meeting for Thursday.'

Another, more urgent message was sent, and again Jimmy replied in the negative saying, 'Wife gone shopping in Newry. I'm doing a deal. Must wait at home for at least two hours. Sorry, will contact soonest.'

Now was the time for action, urgent action. Caution was thrown to the wind. Both the FRU and MI5 knew this could now be a race against time, a race in which vital minutes might be the difference between success and failure. And the consequences of failure for Agent Jimmy personally, as well as the likely consequences to Britain's entire intelligence network in the vital area of south Armagh, would be devastating. They were convinced that the Provos must be on the verge of sending their men to arrest Jimmy and, come what may, they had to get to him first.

Twelve members of J Troop, SAS, who were on duty that day at RAF Aldergrove, were immediately scrambled, ordered to take the

SAS-dedicated helicopter to Bessbrook and wait for instructions. Within ten minutes of receiving their initial order to scramble, they were airborne and heading south. They were warned to prepare for a possible fire-fight with the IRA in south Armagh. Six members of J Troop were told to go in civvies while the others were to go fully armed, blacked-out and in battle fatigues. Details of the mission would be given later at Bessbrook but their objective was the rescue of a man whom must not be permitted to fall into the hands of the IRA, come what may.

Jimmy was living with his young wife in a mobile home near Dundalk while a house was being constructed for them nearby. On occasions Jimmy himself helped out with the basic construction work, like digging the foundations and other labouring work. It helped keep the costs down. His home was in fact six miles south of the border in the Irish Republic, which was, of course, officially out of bounds to the British Army and especially the SAS, which had frequently been accused of violating the Irish Republic's territory.

On this occasion, however, the decision was taken by the TCG that the fate of Agent Jimmy would take precedence. If J Troop needed to cross the border, land their choppers in the Republic, engage in a fire-fight in the area, then they were given permission to do so. The diplomatic niceties would be thrashed out later. The rescue of this FRU agent was all that mattered.

In an effort to save Agent Jimmy, the decision was taken to make a two-pronged attack on his home. Six SAS men, all dressed in civvies, took three civilian cars belonging to FRU from their headquarters at Bessbrook and headed south with orders to cross the border using deserted back roads and head for the map reference where Jimmy was building his new home. All six were armed with Heckler & Koch 9mm USP handguns and Heckler & Koch MP5A4 sub-machine guns with 30-round magazines. They were wearing body armour beneath their civvy jackets.

The remainder of J Troop, all armed with pistols and automatic weapons, were put up in the SAS chopper and told to circle the border area prepared to make the dash to Jimmy's house six miles away at a moment's notice. The SAS-dedicated chopper was not only equipped with extra armour as a precaution against small-arms fire from the ground but J Troop also had access to light machine guns with 200-round metal-link belts capable of sustained rapid fire.

After crossing the border, the three SAS cars kept some distance apart so that anyone seeing them would not suspect there was a convoy heading south. The lead car was about one mile ahead of the other two vehicles, which were 200 yards apart. All were in wireless contact with each other and Bessbrook. The TCG also called in a quick reaction force (QRF) of 12 well-armed soldiers who were detailed to patrol along the border roads and be prepared to make a lightning dash south to the reference point if that became necessary. They were also warned to wear body armour and be prepared for a fire-fight with Provo gunmen.

When the SAS lead vehicle approached Jimmy's home, the driver parked behind a low hedge by a gate some 60 yards off the road. They reported back to base that they could see no activity around the house and they had seen no suspect vehicles on the road south from Dundalk. The first vehicle stayed by the gate, guarding the entrance against any possible intruders, while the second and third vehicles went through the gate to the mobile home. Two SAS men went into his home while the others remained in their vehicles watching for any sign of activity from their SAS mates guarding the gate some 60 yards away.

'What the hell's going on?' Jimmy asked, taken aback by the arrival of these men dressed in civvies but carrying light machine guns.

'We've come to pick you up,' said the SAS man in command. 'We have instructions from FRU. We're SAS. We have to move now; the boys are coming to get you. Your cover's been blown.'

At first, Jimmy looked at them, unable to comprehend what was going on. He had never before been in such a dramatic situation and he struggled to fully understand the urgency. After a few seconds, he seemed to suddenly grasp what was going on.

'Half a sec,' he said, 'I'll grab a few things.'

'Make it quick,' said the commander, 'we don't know how much time we've got. We know they're on their way.'

Jimmy grabbed some money and a coat and was ushered out of the door and into the car. He was told to lie on the floor and a blanket was thrown over him. Then the team moved out.

Jimmy heard the SAS man sitting in the passenger seat on the radio: 'We've collected the package. We're heading north.'

Throughout the entire rescue mission there had been almost complete silence in the FRU office in Bessbrook. The atmosphere was tense, expectant, as everyone waited for the SAS to break silence and report the mission a success. Occasionally the silence was broken when someone coughed, others left the room to have a much-needed smoke, some paced up and down unable to keep still. Occasionally a phone rang, interrupting the tension with its shrill ring. Everyone looked up expectantly as the FRU handler picked up the receiver, but he would shake his head to let those around him know that it wasn't the news they were waiting for. To those in the FRU office and at the TCG in Belfast, the 30-minute rescue mission seemed to go on for hours. Occasionally, those SAS men in the chopper overhead would call in and the QRF on the border would report 'no unusual activity'. The longer the wait continued, those experienced FRU officers knew there was a chance that Jimmy would be rescued. When the message came through that the 'package' had been collected, there was an audible sigh and people held their heads in sheer relief. There were no smiles, no self-congratulation, however, for they still weren't sure if Jimmy was out of the woods. Every FRU handler, assistant and clerk, as well as the senior officers, had felt some guilt about what had happened. There was no attempt to shift the blame, only a collective acceptance that the FRU office had 'fucked up' in a way that should never have occurred at any time under any circumstances.

Two FRU handlers had also been sent to the border in a blacked-out van, which they would use to debrief Jimmy as soon as he was handed over by J Troop. They stopped in a deserted spot some five miles north of the border and waited for the SAS convoy to arrive. The SAS chopper overhead was kept in the air, for no one wanted to take the least possible risk until everyone was certain that Jimmy had been rescued and the situation was once again under control. No one was taking any chances.

Throughout the journey from his home to the border, Jimmy was far more concerned about his young bride, who he told his rescuers was shopping in Stewart's supermarket in Newry High Street, oblivious to what had been going on. He told them that they had only been married a few weeks and she had no idea that he was an undercover agent working for the Force Research Unit. Jimmy begged the SAS troops to make a detour to Newry so that he could tell his wife what had happened, but they had no authority to do that. Their task was to deliver Jimmy to his FRU handlers.

They told Jimmy not to worry because the IRA would have no idea of his wife's whereabouts. They assured him that FRU, which had details of the car she was driving, would pick her up before she crossed the border. If possible, Jimmy was informed, they would try to get permission to drive directly to Newry so that he could meet his wife. Nevertheless, Jimmy continued to fret and there was nothing the SAS troops could do to calm his nerves.

As soon as the SAS and young Jimmy reached the FRU handlers in their blacked-out van, the problem of Jimmy's wife was explained. They immediately agreed that everything must be done to contact his wife and prevent her from crossing the border on her way home. The FRU realised, of course, that if the IRA captured Jimmy's wife, she would be used as a pawn in their evil games, and they would threaten to kill her unless Jimmy volunteered to return of his own free will to his home in the south. The FRU handlers and the TCG knew the Provos would happily play such a game with the 20-year-old woman, putting incredible pressure on Jimmy to turn himself over to a certain death. But the FRU could not, and would not, permit such a deal because of the real probability that the torture he would face would be so great that he would squeal. And that was unthinkable.

The FRU handlers in the blacked-out van contacted Bessbrook, explained the situation concerning Jimmy's wife and made two suggestions. They would immediately drive to Newry with Jimmy, because he was the only person who could recognise her. In the meantime, one of the SAS cars would travel towards the border and keep watch on the Newry to Dundalk road along which Jimmy said she would drive. Of course, he gave not only the description and number of the car but also a description of his wife.

So, two FRU handlers accompanied Jimmy to Newry by car and the SAS men in civilian clothes made themselves inconspicuous in and around Stewart's supermarket. The FRU handler carried no weapon but the members of the SAS four-man brick were armed with automatic machine pistols. They made sure they kept in sight of each other just in case trouble broke out.

Jimmy saw his wife as she was pushing her half-laden trolley around the store. She looked shocked to see him, especially as he was accompanied by a total stranger.

'We've got to go, darling,' he said to her, looking agitated.

'What do you mean?' she replied. 'I've still got some shopping to do.'

'You have to leave it; we must go, now. I'll explain everything outside.'

His wife looked mesmerised, as though Jimmy had taken leave of his senses, as he took her arm and half pushed, half frog-marched her past the check-out counter and out of the shop, closely followed by his FRU handler. As soon as they walked out onto the street, the FRU driver spotted them and drove up.

'Get in,' Jimmy said to his wife as he opened the door, and the two clambered into the back. The FRU handler got into the front passenger seat and they drove away north out of Newry. When they were out of the town, the FRU handler radioed, 'Package collected; heading back to base.'

It was after receiving this message that the atmosphere in Bessbrook Mill changed perceptibly and people began to relax.

But the mood in the FRU car was still fraught, for Jimmy's wife had not the slightest idea what was going on, where they were going or who the two strangers were in the car.

'What's going on? What's happening? Where are we going?' she kept asking.

Jimmy would tell her to calm down, saying, 'I'll explain everything to you when we stop. But this isn't the time or the place.'

'Tell me now,' she persisted. 'I want to know what's going on and I want to go home. What's happening? What the fuck's happening? For God's sake, tell me what's going on!'

Jimmy asked his FRU handler if they could stop at Banbridge to buy some booze and fags, which he believed his wife was badly in need of to calm her nerves. He wanted her to be in a receptive mood when he told the truth of what was going on and why they were travelling away from their home with two strangers. When they stopped in Banbridge town centre, the FRU handler and Jimmy went to the local supermarket where Jimmy bought vodka, coke, eight large cans of lager and forty cigarettes. The rest of the journey to Palace Army Barracks was quieter as Jimmy and his young wife drank some booze and chain-smoked.

The couple were shown to a former married quarters in the barracks, which was well-furnished with all mod cons. It was like a hotel. There were two bedrooms, one with a double bed, a good-sized smart living room with a TV, a kitchen stocked with essentials, central heating and constant hot water. Jimmy and his wife were left there to chat for a couple of hours and Jimmy was given a phone number he could use if he wanted to call his FRU handler.

They stayed in the married quarters for a week to let Jimmy's wife take in everything her husband had told her and to explain their alternatives. Of course, Jimmy was debriefed by his FRU agents, but his days as a spy were over forever. The couple agreed to take the advice of Jimmy's FRU handlers and arrangements were made for them to move to a safe house in England. Later they were provided with new identities, the British Government bought them a small house and nine months later Jimmy's bride gave birth to a little boy. She had conceived during their week in Palace Barracks.

In another dramatic rescue, Scappaticci saved the life of a young Territorial Army soldier who was working undercover in Belfast in 1984. The soldier was caught up in rioting in the Ardoyne in a pitched battle between Catholics and Protestants in which bricks were hurled, vehicles set alight, petrol bombs exchanged and many young people injured as the two arch enemies clashed repeatedly at close quarters, using bicycle chains, batons, sticks and broken bottles to inflict injuries. During the street fighting which took place either side of burning barricades, Catholic street vigilantes captured a lad who they believed was one of the Protestant rioters who had been attacking them. They took him to a house, searched him and found a current British Territorial Army ID card in his shoe. Realising they might have discovered a British Army spy, the Catholic kids sent for a well-known hardline Belfast Provo with a fierce reputation.

He interrogated the young soldier and also came to the conclusion that the young man was probably a British spy working for Military Intelligence. Scap was informed by the IRA of the capture of a possible spy and called to interrogate the soldier to establish the truth. Before answering the call to go to the Ardoyne, however, Scap put in a quick call to his FRU handler telling them what had happened and the exact address to which he had been told to report to question the soldier.

The TCG then made the decision to mount an operation to rescue the unknown soldier, primarily because they were aware that at that time some British infantrymen were being used to infiltrate Catholic gangs and report back information of names and descriptions of the young ringleaders.

Within 30 minutes, a platoon of 12 well-armed British soldiers had arrived in armoured cars, surrounded the house where the soldier was being held and arrested everyone inside. The soldier was rescued unharmed. No Provo seemed to suspect that Scap had been responsible for the tip-off, which most certainly saved the soldier's life.

Yet another young man, another FRU undercover agent, owed his life to Freddie Scappaticci after he came under suspicion from the Provisional IRA. This young man, known as 'Agent Six-one-one-two' (6112), lived in the Ardoyne and held a lowly position within the Provisional IRA. Quiet, unassuming and somewhat reticent, he was being bullied and kicked around by his so-called Provo mates, who took advantage of the fact that he accepted his position and was prepared to carry out whatever lowly duties were assigned to him.

And then one day he was selected for further interrogation after being stopped at a FRU vehicle checkpoint and taken away for questioning in the traditional FRU screening process. It was during his interview with FRU handlers that the lad let slip the way he was being treated by his Provo mates and it became obvious that he was not at all happy with his situation. The FRU handlers saw a chink of doubt which they decided to exploit.

He was invited to return for another chat and within 28 days Agent 6112 had agreed to work undercover for the Force Research Unit. He was advised to push for a job within the local Ardoyne Provo unit and within a couple of months he was appointed their quartermaster with responsibility for storing explosives. From the FRU's perspective this was a prime job, because they knew it would be possible to arrange for some of these explosives and their detonators to be spiked.

And that's what happened. The explosives then being used by the Ardoyne Provos were nicknamed 'annie': ammonia nitrate was made from farm fertiliser. The detonators were usually commercial gelignite or C4, a military type of plastic explosive. But these fertiliser 'annies' required a really powerful charge to trigger the explosion and the detonators were simply not man enough for the job. They were always failing to explode, but as the Provo leaders did not understand that the equipment was not up to the task they were constantly looking for scapegoats to blame for the failures.

To a certain extent, of course, the IRA leadership was right to question why the home-made bombs were failing to explode. Whenever the Provos were planning a bomb attack, 6112 would be told to hand over the necessary equipment for the Provo bomb team to assemble and he would contact his FRU handler and inform them. E4A, the RUC's covert surveillance unit, would be alerted and they would secretly visit 6112's bomb store, tamper with the detonator to make it less powerful, thus making the chances of setting off a powerful explosion extremely unlikely. After more than eight of these bombs failed to explode, the Provos became suspicious and called 6112 to an interrogation.

On this occasion, 6112 was questioned by his Provo mates within his own unit, and his answers to their questions were sufficiently convincing that he was permitted to go free. Some weeks later, however, after more bombs failed to explode, he was again called in for questioning. This time the Provos called in Scap and asked him to put real pressure on the lad to discover if he was telling the truth. The Provos had convinced themselves that their young quartermaster was a traitor, but they could not prove it. They knew that Scap, with his fearsome reputation for making traitors squeal and beg for mercy, was the man to discover the truth. They explained as much to Scap before inviting him to question the young man.

The young quartermaster was told he had to go south of the border and he knew that meant he would more than likely face torture and really rough questioning. All young Provo volunteers knew that being ordered south meant the leadership were convinced the volunteer had become a traitor to the cause. The vast majority of members of the Provisional IRA also knew of Scap's role within the organisation: they understood that he was a fierce interrogator who was quite prepared to resort to torture to ensure he discovered the truth. They also knew of his favourite torture technique. This was to all but drown the victim in a bath of cold water. A soaking wet towel would be wrapped around the head of the victim as he knelt over the side of a bath full of water, his ankles tied together, his hands handcuffed behind his back. One man would hold the victim while a second would force his head under the water until he fell unconscious and ceased to struggle. But that wasn't the end of the matter. The victim would then be lifted out of the water, but the sodden towel would be left wrapped around his head. The Provos had discovered that on most occasions the victim would then slowly regain consciousness, though he would be still fighting for breath. This was the time that the questioning began once again and Scap had found that it was at this point that most men broke their silence and confessed. Provo volunteers therefore knew if they entered a bathroom and saw a bath full to the brim with water, then they would be subjected to the infamous water torture unless, of course, they chose to confess. They also knew that the moment they confessed to betraying the IRA cause they were dead men.

The Provo leadership never wanted suspects to be killed accidentally, because, if the suspect died before confessing, his information would go to the grave. The leadership always wanted to know every detail of the confession to discover exactly what had been going on and, more importantly, details and descriptions of contacts or handlers within the security service. Scap understood their requirements and his claim to fame was that nine times out of ten his methods of torture produced the required result: a compliant victim who confessed all.

On this occasion, however, Scap came to the young man's rescue. He informed the local Provo commander that he could not go south for 24 hours because he was too heavily involved and, as a result, the Provo leadership decided to wait. It was useful in such rescue missions that Scap's demands were nearly always accepted by Provo commanders because they realised his power amongst the upper echelons of the leadership. On this occasion, Scap immediately made contact with his FRU handlers and told them that he was to be sent south to question a young quartermaster whom the Provos believed was spiking their explosives. He told them that they had perhaps just 24 hours to save his life.

After a brief meeting at FRU headquarters, the decision was taken to save 6112's life. They called him to an urgent meeting that evening and said it was imperative that he attend. They knew that 6112 had a wife and four young children and they lived in the Ardoyne. As soon as 6112 arrived for his meeting, he was immediately informed of the desperate situation he was facing.

'What can I do?' asked 6112 in desperation. 'I've got a wife and four kids at home. If I go down south, they will be OK. But if I fuck off, they might be treated as traitors and I couldn't let that happen to them. I could never live with myself if I left them behind to survive in a community where everyone knew that I was a traitor. I know how people can react in these circumstances. The lives of my wife and my kids would be hell. I couldn't do that to them.'

His FRU handler told him to relax, quieten down. 'You won't have to. We can arrange to fly you, your wife and all the kids to the mainland tonight. You will be all together and safe. The IRA won't have the faintest knowledge where you are. We will look after the whole family. What do you say?'

'How will we live?' he asked.

'We'll take care of that. Don't worry. Now, do you want to go?'

'Shit, yes,' he said, 'but I don't know what the wife will say.'

'Don't worry,' his handler told him, 'we will explain everything to her.'

Two hours later, under cover of darkness, 6112 and two handlers drove to 6112's home in the Ardoyne in an unmarked Transit van. There was also an armed guard in the van. The two handlers and 6112 went inside and together they explained everything to his young wife, who, by the end of the conversation, was visibly shaking with fear. She asked some questions which the handlers answered, trying to reassure her that all would be fine.

'What can we take with us?' she asked despairingly.

'Nothing, save some clothes in a couple of suitcases and any personal keepsakes,' she was told. 'The rest you must leave behind. We have five minutes only. They may already be on their way here.'

The four kids were woken and dressed while 6112 raced around the house picking up a few odds and ends and stuffing some clothes in two large suitcases. Then, while one handler checked the road outside was quiet and clear, the family and the handlers made their way out of their house and into the van. Standing guard in the shadows was the armed officer. One hour later the van pulled up at RAF Aldergrove and 6112, his wife and their four children were taken to a Lear jet that had been made ready for their escape. Two hours later they landed at a military airport in the south of England and were taken to a hotel for the night. Their names and identities were changed, they were provided with a furnished house and 6112 was found a job. The family never returned to Belfast. Once again Scap had come to the rescue.

There were many other occasions when Freddie Scappaticci came to the rescue of undercover agents working for FRU, MI5 and also the RUC Special Branch. But, understandably, he had to take the greatest care, for he could never risk blowing his identity. Preserving Steak Knife's cover led to the deaths of several innocent people. The Force Research Unit would be given permission to organise the killing of another man if that was absolutely necessary to protect Steak Knife's identity. One such killing occurred on 9 October 1987, when Francisco Notarantonio, a 66-

year-old pensioner of Italian extraction who had lived in Northern Ireland all his life, was taken out by a Loyalist gang working under instructions from the Force Research Unit.

Notarantonio was one of the old-style Republicans, a member of the Official IRA going back some 50 years. During the late 1940s he was jailed for involvement in so-called anti-British activities. He had also been picked up during the internment sweep of the 1970s and spent time in detention. But following internment, Notarantonio was brushed aside by the young Provo thrusters and, while still a staunch Republican, he decided to retire, though he continued to be a frequent visitor to Republican clubs and pubs.

In 1987, however, word somehow got around the Provo network that there was a mature member of the Republican movement in Belfast who was working for the British security services. It was rumoured that he was a foreigner and probably of Italian extraction. In a desperate move to allay the suspicion that Steak Knife was in the frame, the decision was taken at the highest level within the Force Research Unit, and agreed by MI5, that something, anything, had to be done to protect Steak Knife's identity. Someone remembered poor old Francisco and decided that on this occasion he would fit the bill perfectly.

It was decided that Notarantonio's life would have to be sacrificed to save Steak Knife. A killing was decreed and orders were given to a Loyalist terror squad to carry out the murder. Notarantonio's exact address in Whitecliffe Parade in the Ballymurphy district of west Belfast was provided, identity pictures of the man were handed over, and RUC and army patrols which had been present in the area around Whitecliffe Parade the day before were withdrawn.

Shortly after half past seven on the morning of 9 October 1987, Notarantonio and his wife were sleeping in their bed when four hooded gunmen, wearing dark boiler suits, arrived outside their home in a Vauxhall Cavalier. Two jumped out of the car and kicked down the front door in seconds. They ran up the stairs and stormed into the old couple's bedroom. The two pensioners were still lying side by side in their bed. It made no difference that they were too old to defend themselves or take any evasive action. The two gunmen opened fire at close range with handguns, hitting Notarantonio in the chest as he struggled to get out of the bed to tackle his attackers. The force of the shots swung the old man round and the gunman then fired shots into his back. It is believed he died instantly. His wife was unharmed but badly shocked. The gunmen then fled. The killing had taken less than a minute. The car, which had been hijacked that morning in the Woodvale area of Belfast, was later found abandoned at Blackmountain Way in the Springmartin area. Police found no clues in the vehicle. The killers, of course, were never traced. But that murder of an innocent pensioner was deemed a great success by the intelligence services, for the Provos seemed to believe that Notarantonio had been the suspected guilty informant and he had been removed for ever. Scappaticci was never told that this killing had been undertaken to save his skin.

Scappaticci was always known, and is still recognised, as a quiet man. He is the sort of person who could easily be lost in a crowd, who would never draw attention to himself under any circumstances. He always kept his cool, never seemed to become excited or agitated. He would always go about his work in a quiet, methodical manner, even his work as an interrogator or torturer. He preferred to keep his own counsel and stay in the shadows, and would hardly ever become involved in a discussion, let alone an argument. He also wouldn't suffer fools gladly, but would simply move away from them rather than argue or discuss the matter that had been raised. Scap was never known to shout, but he did swear and he would often simply nod when asked a question rather than saying 'yes'. Of course, he may not have been such a bland person in his youth and it may well be that his extraordinary long career as an agent caused him to adopt this self-effacing image of anonymity. In any case, it worked. Freddie Scappaticci never told his Italian wife or his children that he was working for the British

Government. They believed that he was simply working in the family fish and chip shop. He put down his frequent absences from Belfast to business, the necessity of him having to travel around Ireland securing fish supplies. (The wags at British Military Intelligence suggested the pseudonym Steak Knife because he worked in a fish and chip shop and they believed this would throw people off the scent.)

It is very difficult to assess accurately the contribution that Scap made to the eventual peace in Northern Ireland, but it is true that he made an extraordinary difference to the British Government's methods of fighting the war against the IRA and the other terrorist organisations. Scap knew what was going on amongst the highest echelons of the Provisional IRA and it was the thinking, the machinations, the political manoeuvrings of the Provo and Sinn Fein leaders that were of such prime importance to MI5, the senior civil servants and British politicians who had to deal with the problems thrown up. But he also made it his business to keep his finger on the pulse of the Provos' plans for launching bombing raids and other major attacks in the hope that he might be able to on-pass the intelligence quickly enough that action could be taken to thwart them.

On several occasions, planned IRA bomb attacks on the British mainland came to nought because Scap forewarned the British authorities via his FRU handlers of the impending attacks. But at other times Scap heard only sketchy details of possible attacks being planned. Sometimes those plans ended in the Provos launching devastating attacks both on the mainland and, more frequently, in Belfast. Understandably, he had to take the greatest care that he didn't ask too many questions, perhaps arousing suspicion. His orders were to do nothing whatsoever that might reveal his role as a British spy.

Sir John Stevens has made a request to the head of MI5 that he be permitted to interview Steak Knife concerning all the matters which his team have been investigating for nearly a decade. Sir

John hopes that Scap might be able to provide some information about the allegations of collusion between the security services and Loyalist paramilitaries. But at the time of writing, MI5 are understood to be still considering the request and no final decision has yet been made.

Indeed, from the seven years of enquiries this author has been making concerning collusion, it seems unlikely that Steak Knife would, in fact, be able to cast any light on the subject. After examining the work Scap did throughout his years of involvement with British Intelligence, it appears that he never came into direct contact with any Loyalist paramilitaries nor did he have access to any of their secret operations or contacts with British Intelligence.

It is known that MI5 does not want Scap involved in any inquiries by the Stevens team nor any other authority investigating what went on in Northern Ireland throughout the Troubles. It is feared that such investigations might become politically embarrassing not only to Scap but also to British Intelligence. This author knows, too, that Freddie Scappaticci has no wish whatsoever to face questioning from any authority and MI5 would not want to push him into having to face such questioning on any security matters.

Today, Freddie Scappaticci maintains the stance he has taken since the Steak Knife affair burst into the public domain. He staunchly maintains that he is not the man known as Steak Knife and that those who suggest he is are mistaken.

He now divides his time between Belfast and southern Italy, where members of his extended family live. He has not yet decided for certain to where he intends to retire but it is thought that, as a fluent Italian speaker, he might eventually return to the land of his forefathers and forget all about the man the world now knows as Steak Knife.

Chapter Five

NELSON – THE DOUBLE AGENT

The recruitment of Brian Nelson was another vital coup by British Military Intelligence, and occurred only as the result of a very drunk Nelson becoming angry with a senior officer in the Loyalist Ulster Defence Association who had tried to take liberties with Nelson's attractive young wife following a Christmas party.

The alleged attempted rape of his wife took place on Christmas Day 1985, and an angry, alcohol-fuelled Nelson was determined to get even with the UDA – the organisation for which he then claimed he was working as an intelligence officer. Shortly before 5 a.m. on a bitterly cold, rainswept night, Nelson had trudged half-drunk through the dark streets of New Barnsley and presented himself outside the fortress-type building occupied jointly by the army and the RUC.

He stood, soaked to the skin, under the bright security lights in front of the large metal gates and tried to fathom out how to get inside the building. Dressed in black winkle-pickers, white shirt, thin black trousers and a three-quarter-length grey and black checked coat, the dishevelled, bruised and unshaven Nelson had the look of a man who had slept rough that night or not at all.

He began to shout, trying to raise the attention of someone behind the imposing gates, but there was no reply. After several minutes of this, he became impatient and annoyed at the lack of response. Suddenly, however, a side gate opened and a young soldier armed and wearing a flak jacket motioned him to come over.

As Nelson walked through the gate, the soldier asked him what he was doing there. In a slurred voice, Nelson explained that he wanted to see someone from British Military Intelligence. That was an unusual request at any time, but at 5 a.m. on Boxing Day morning it seemed positively bizarre to the guard on duty, who, understandably, assumed that he was probably talking to some drunken fool who would come to his senses in a few hours and, hopefully, disappear home feeling the worse for wear.

When the guard pressed him further, Nelson refused to give him any more information, saying that he would only speak to someone from Military Intelligence. Somewhat reluctantly, the soldier nodded agreement and took Nelson to the police sergeant on duty. After checking Nelson's name and address on the computer, the duty sergeant warned Nelson that he would have to be searched, hoping this might persuade the unkempt drunk swaying in front of him to forget his plan and toddle off. But Nelson was compliant, raising his arms and spreading his legs as though he was used to such an order. The soldier checked him out thoroughly, running his hands over his arms, legs and body, searching his pockets and even making Nelson take off his shoes and socks so they too could be examined. But they found nothing.

In another effort to dissuade Nelson from hanging around, the sergeant warned him that he would have to wait two or three hours before he could see anyone from British Military Intelligence, as he wasn't sure what time they would come on duty on Boxing Day.

In response, Nelson gave the sergeant his name and his former regimental number from the time he had served in the British

Army with the Black Watch. He also told them that he was now an intelligence officer with the Ulster Defence Association. On hearing those two pieces of information, the sergeant became more interested in his bizarre visitor, offering him a warming cup of tea and a hot bacon sandwich. Nelson gulped the tea and ate the sandwich with gusto. Both seemed to help his parched mouth, thumping headache and shaking hands, which he was unable to hold steady.

Some four hours later, a jaded-looking Nelson was sitting in front of two burly army sergeants in a small, bare interview room about ten feet by eight feet, with only a single radiator for warmth. Before agreeing to interview Nelson, the two sergeants had read the computer print-out on him giving his name, his age – thirty-six – and the fact that he was a former member of the Ulster Volunteer Force (UVF), the fiercely Loyalist Protestant terrorist organisation. Nelson's army record appeared abysmal, portraying him as an unreliable soldier who refused to obey orders, frequently appeared on company orders for misdemeanours and, as a result, during his short army career, had spent several hours in the glasshouse (military detention barracks). Unhappy, undisciplined and a poor soldier who frequently went AWOL, Nelson had been discharged in 1969. In 1975, he had been jailed for five years for possession of arms and explosives. On his release from prison three years later, he had immediately joined the UDA, and, in 1980, had been appointed one of the organisation's intelligence officers.

After running through his embarrassing military record with the sergeants, a rather shamefaced Nelson told them he had information that they might find useful. Then he seemed to perk up, demanding of the two men whether they were in fact from Military Intelligence.

On confirming their status, the sergeants queried why Nelson appeared to be so concerned. His response was that he didn't trust the RUC or Special Branch, giving as evidence the fact that he had walked through a Catholic area in the cold and the rain that morning to ensure he would be speaking to Military Intelligence and not the police. In answer to further questioning, Nelson explained that he would never talk to the RUC or the Special Branch because he was certain his identity and the information he was providing would immediately be relayed back to the UDA.

This answer persuaded both men that Nelson just might be worth listening to further. Gently, they began to press him as to what information he possessed that might help them. But Nelson chose to ignore those questions. He had his own agenda and kept repeating that the reason he had come to the station was that he wanted to get even with both the UDA and the UVF.

When asked why he was seeking revenge, in a quiet, matter-of-fact voice Nelson told the two men what had happened to his wife, describing the events of the UDA party on the Silverstream estate. He explained that his wife Jean had been with him along with some 40 other guests, drinking, chatting and making merry. He told how one or two couples were dancing while others simply got drunk.

He then came to the meat of the problem, explaining, 'This particular man kept dancing with my Jean, flirting with her, trying to smooch her, feeling her up – you know the sort of thing.

'I didn't mind at first and continued to drink until I began to feel a bit pissed. I suggested we should go home after she told me she had drunk enough and was feeling a bit unwell. This man volunteered to walk both of us back home and it seemed a good idea, as I was feeling legless. When we got home, we felt better – the fresh air must have helped. I was in the kitchen fixing some drinks when I heard Jean scream. At first I took no notice, thinking they were just larking about. Then I heard her shout, "No, no, no, get off!" and I guessed he was trying it on.

'I ran in and this bloke was lying on top of her, trying to screw her. Her dress was halfway up her body and he was trying to force himself on top of her, pulling at her knickers, while she was trying to push him away. I exploded, yelling at him, asking him what the fuck he thought he was doing, trying to screw my wife.'

The man told Nelson to 'Fuck off back to the kitchen' and leave them alone, claiming that he and Jean were just having some fun. But Nelson could see the look of anger and disgust on his wife's face, and, understandably, he was upset and angry.

He tried to pull the man off his wife, yelling at him, 'Just having fun? You're trying to rape my wife.'

The shouting match between the two men ended in a fistfight, with Nelson coming off worse. The man then stormed out of the house, closely followed by a furious Nelson whose pride had been wounded by the beating the heavily built man had inflicted on him. Back at the party, Nelson confronted senior UDA officers, demanding they should discipline the man for attempting to rape his wife. At first they took it as a joke that had gone wrong, but the more Nelson persisted in his demands the less interested they became. They were enjoying a party; they had all had a few drinks and it was Christmas. They didn't want to know about Nelson's personal problems. In no uncertain terms, they told Nelson that such an allegation of rape by a UDA man was not the concern of the organisation and they wanted nothing to do with it.

The two intelligence officers looked at each other and, without saying a word, both understood that Nelson might indeed be worth nurturing as a potential informant. Plainly, he was a hurt, angry man who wanted to get even with those UDA leaders who had dismissed what he believed was a serious allegation against one of their own men.

Nelson then offered the two army sergeants a deal, saying that whatever information they required from the UDA, he would readily supply. Now they really became interested, but they didn't show it. They let Nelson have his head so that they could judge his anger. He raged at them, describing the entire leadership as 'a load of bastards'. When he had finished, one of the sergeants told him, 'I think we can do business.'

At last Nelson calmed down and appeared relieved that the

intelligence officers had apparently taken his allegations seriously. He told them, 'Whatever you want me to do, I'll do it.'

When they had shaken hands, one sergeant asked Nelson, 'If the UDA wouldn't help, why didn't you go to the police and report the incident?'

'The peelers?' Nelson said, raising his voice in mock surprise. 'Fuck off! A man with my record go to the police and complain? You must be fuckin' nuts. They would have just kicked me out of the station. Don't you realise the RUC are in it up to the hilt with the UDA and the UVF? They provide the Loyalists with all their information.'

The officers then decided to check Nelson's credentials by asking him a few questions about the UDA. Nelson's answers would reveal exactly how up-to-date his knowledge of the UDA really was. They asked him a series of questions about the hierarchy of the UDA and the UVF and about recent changes in the leaderships. His answers impressed them, suggesting strongly that he knew a great deal about both organisations. That satisfied both officers. They had by now heard enough to realise that the bruised, scruffy-looking little man sitting in front of them might just be a useful contact.

They told him to go away and in a week's time he was to phone a number they gave him and ask for Mick. They told him to keep the number to himself and tell no one of his visit that morning. When Nelson left the station that morning, the two handlers had no idea whether he might change his ideas when he sobered up, in which case they would never hear from him again.

Brian Nelson was an Ulsterman born and bred. He had two brothers and a sister, attended primary and secondary school in Belfast, and in 1965, at the age of fifteen, left school without a single qualification. His father, a shipyard worker, arranged for the teenage Brian to begin four years' training as a joiner, but after eighteen months, Nelson became bored with the job and quit.

He fancied becoming a soldier and joined the Black Watch, but he was unable to cope with either the discipline or the rigorous training. Brian Nelson had a problem – he couldn't and he wouldn't take orders. He was constantly going AWOL before being picked up by the police and returned to his regiment. As a result of such poor discipline, Nelson spent many months paying for his belligerence, peeling potatoes, scrubbing floors, weeding gardens, sweeping the parade ground and painting coal white. Fed up with such a poor recruit, the Black Watch got rid of him in 1969. He was just 19.

Nelson returned to Belfast at about the time the Northern Ireland Civil Rights Association was about to be forced into the background by the IRA. Protestant Loyalists realised that they might need to defend their areas once again from Republicans demanding the whole of Ireland should be a single Republican state. Nelson joined the nascent Ulster Protestant Volunteers (UPV), the plan behind which was to establish groups on every Protestant housing estate in Belfast to act as a defence unit in case of attack from Catholics.

Everyone who joined signed a form stating their name, address, age, occupation and, more importantly, whether they had any experience in the police, army, fire brigade or medical services. Brian Nelson, allegedly a veteran private in the British Army, was exactly the type of experienced young man the UPV wanted. Many of those who joined the new UPV later became members of the UDA.

About this time, Brian Nelson met and married his pretty teenage Belfast girlfriend, who was from a sound Protestant family. Bright, sexy, impetuous and fun, Jean, then only 17, was swept off her feet and within a matter of months they were married. In time, Brian and Jean Nelson would have four children and would live on the all-Protestant Silverstream estate in the Shankill area of Belfast. They rented their small, unpretentious home from the Northern Ireland Housing Executive.

Membership of the UPV garnered respect for Nelson, something he had always yearned for but never before won. He was able to turn his dubious military experience to his advantage and was welcomed as an expert in weapons training, having undergone basic training using rifles and Bren guns. He did at least know how to drill and march, knew the basics of field training and camouflage, and he had learned how to survive forced marches.

The young, totally inexperienced recruits looked up to Nelson, seeing him as a 'veteran'. Within months he was promoted to street defence leader, a sort of NCO, in charge of the street in which he lived – organising meetings, exercises, drill and weapons training – and in charge of discipline. He revelled in his newly elevated status and during the next few years would become almost authoritarian, not only to the recruits but also to others in the organisation.

When patrolling the streets of Protestant north Belfast, Nelson and his defence unit would wear masks and carry pickaxe handles. As a status symbol, Nelson would carry a .22 starting pistol. In 1975, he was arrested and charged with possession of three handguns and three sub-machine guns, as well as a small amount of explosives. It was suggested at the time that he might have been acting as one of the UDA's quartermasters. He was sentenced to five years in prison but with good behaviour he was out again in 1978, when the sectarian war was at its height. That three-year jail term, however, had given Nelson everything he yearned for – status within the Loyalist movement.

Some two weeks after Nelson's Boxing Day chat with the Military Intelligence NCOs, he returned of his own free will to meet his two handlers. They were still not absolutely certain whether Nelson was genuine, but they were so desperate to forge relationships with anyone inside the UDA that they were prepared to take the risk. They were under considerable pressure from senior officers of the Joint Irish Section – in reality MI5's operation in Northern Ireland – to infiltrate Loyalist organisations. All their intelligence suggested

Loyalists were buying arms, explosives and ammunition from overseas; streamlining their organisation into a fighting force with real capability; and recruiting and training as many Protestants as possible. MI5 needed to know exactly how serious the Loyalist threat had become.

But all Nelson's bravado and talk of his role 'at the heart' of the UDA produced very little intelligence and none of any consequence save for the training schedules of UDA gunmen and details of their weapons, firearms and bomb-making capabilities which were already known. To the FRU, this was a pathetic waste of their time.

In March 1986, Nelson suddenly announced he was going to Munich in Germany to work for a Belfast floor-laying firm with whom he had done odd-jobs through the years. Instead of being .perturbed by the loss of an agent, British Military Intelligence was, in fact, relieved he had gone. Six months later, however, Nelson made the phone call that would change his life for ever, when he called his handlers back in Belfast and told them of a planned South African arms deal that he was about to negotiate on behalf of the UDA.

FRU officers informed MI5 and Nelson was persuaded to fly to South Africa via London, for which he would be handsomely paid. He agreed, and after talks with MI5 officers Nelson said he would return to Germany from South Africa via London and report on his talks with his South African contacts. Nelson kept his part of the bargain and MI5 told FRU of the arms deal Nelson had set up on behalf of the UDA.

It was following Nelson's trip to South Africa that British Military Intelligence and MI5 fell out over him. The reason: both wanted to recruit Nelson to work for them. And both intelligence organisations were prepared to break their own strict codes of conduct to try and recruit him. Nelson was now hot property.

Within the space of a week, both Military Intelligence and MI5 officers flew to Germany with bids asking him to join their organisation. And yet, according to Home Office and Ministry of Defence regulations, neither MI5 nor British Military Intelligence was permitted to recruit agents overseas. Further than that, no FRU personnel were permitted to operate outside Northern Ireland and neither were agents or officers of MI5 permitted to operate outside Britain, except under exceptional circumstances and then only with permission. No such permission had been sought.

At their Munich meeting, Military Intelligence offered Nelson a deal: £300 a week in cash, a reasonable but not a flash saloon car, a house in Belfast and a cover – a job as a taxi driver. Without a moment's hesitation, Nelson said yes and shook hands on the deal. He seemed really elated at the prospect of working as an undercover agent for British Military Intelligence again.

At that time Nelson did not tell the Military Intelligence officers that the UDA had already offered him a job back home in Belfast as their chief intelligence officer. This was to be an official salaried position because he had handled the South African arms deal so professionally. And Military Intelligence did not tell Nelson that they had known of his new job with the UDA before they had flown out to persuade him to work undercover for them. Indeed, one of the main reasons FRU were so desperate to recruit Nelson was the fact that, as the UDA's chief intelligence officer, he would be in the best position possible to know exactly what was going on in the Loyalists' most powerful military outfit.

Nelson was further taken aback when the MI5 officer he had met in London arrived unannounced on his Munich doorstep and, with another MI5 man present, tried to sweet-talk him into working for them. Indeed, MI5's desperation to recruit Nelson became apparent when details of their offer became known. MI5 offered Nelson a job for life, almost unheard of for an undercover agent. He was to be given the pay of a middle-ranking MI5 officer, a generous civil service pension, expenses, a car and a house in Belfast.

But Nelson had his doubts about working for MI5. He would later tell one of his FRU handlers that, although the MI5 offer was 'brilliant', he simply didn't trust them. Nelson feared that after agreeing to work for MI5 they might renege on the deal and leave him high and dry, whereas he had more faith that Military Intelligence would fulfil their side of the bargain. He felt he could trust the army. Nelson also feared that MI5 might go further and inform their contacts inside the UDA that he was now on their payroll. Another reason for turning down MI5 was the simple fact that Nelson felt uncomfortable when talking to the two MI5 men who had interviewed him, for they spoke with upper-class English accents and behaved too politely. Nelson felt awkward and inferior in their presence. He explained later, 'I thought at the time they'd never last a pint of lager in a Belfast pub before everyone knew who they were.'

After his return to Belfast to start his new jobs as the UDA's chief intelligence officer and a British spy, the Force Research Unit had found Nelson and his young family a house, provided them with a car and the latest computer so that he could organise a database of Republican and Sinn Fein members as a front for his job with the UDA. With help from MI5 and MI6, the FRU had organised with German intelligence for it to be reported that Nelson had won £30,000 (worth £70,000 in 2004) on a German lottery game so that his return to Belfast and the down-payment on a small house and purchasing a second-hand car would not seem unreasonable to his friends in the UDA. The FRU had also arranged for Nelson's photograph and lottery win to be publicised in a local German paper so that Nelson could take back the newspaper cutting to show friends, the UDA and others proof of his good fortune.

FRU officers were initially impressed with his enthusiasm and efficiency, and were pleasantly surprised when Nelson arrived for one of his secret meetings in a safe house with a bulging briefcase containing UDA intelligence material, including 'mug shots' of people which looked as though they had originated from RUC or

Ulster Defence Regiment files. Some files even included the secret P-cards used by the RUC. These were 'personality' cards which contained all the person's details, including name, address, names of wife and children, make of car and registration number, National Insurance number, any convictions and prison records, political affiliations and facts about any political activities, as well as involvement, or suspected involvement, in any terrorist organisation. Of course, these cards should never have reached the officers of the UDA.

At that meeting, Nelson produced full details of some 200 people from all areas of the Province, though the majority were from Belfast. Most files were of Provo, INLA and Sinn Fein activists, supporters and sympathisers; some were old and useless but the majority were up to date.

Nelson's handlers offered to sort out the portfolio of names, addresses, phone numbers, car numbers and other details for him. In reality, of course, they wanted to check and cross-check all the details, as well as keeping copies for their own files.

Two or three times a week throughout that summer and autumn, Nelson would meet his FRU handlers at various locations, for their keen new recruit was intent on putting as much information as possible on the computer which the FRU had given him. He kept the computer, unsecured, in a bedroom at his home. Nelson told his handlers that he wanted a comprehensive database of Republican activists, Provo gunmen and bombers, as well as Sinn Fein politicians and party members. And the FRU even went so far as to assist Nelson in compiling his database with files from their own secret computers, providing facts that he could not discover from his UDA sources. By September 1987, Nelson's computerised database was described as 'comprehensive' by FRU handlers. Nelson was learning fast.

The Force Research Unit had now reached a situation in which they knew what was going on at the most senior levels of the Provisional IRA via their super-spy Steak Knife, and they were also gaining some idea of what the Loyalist UDA were planning via Nelson. With the work being carried out by Box on the political level and the twin undercover agents deep inside the Provos and the UDA, British Intelligence had finally reached a stage where they were quietly confident they might shortly be in a position to have some influence and control over events unfolding on both sides of the religious divide.

At this time, the Force Research Unit was divided into three sectors – East Det, based in Belfast, North Det based in Derry and South Det based in Bessbrook, near Newry – and could boast of some 70 handlers, 20 collators and another 20 back-up clerks. Handlers would routinely report to their senior officers on how their various touts and agents were working, giving details of all the intelligence they were providing. These reports would usually carry information from the handlers on how their agents were performing, and the quality of the intelligence provided, as well as their commitment to the job.

The task of a good handler is to win the confidence of the agents and touts they are running, to understand the difficulties facing their agents, to separate the good human intelligence from the poor, and to keep up their agents' morale so that they will continue to provide the intelligence so very necessary in such a conflict. In Northern Ireland, good handlers were the intelligence services' greatest assets.

The head of the FRU at this time was Lieutenant Colonel Gordon Kerr. Kerr hailed from the Aberdeen area of Scotland and was a graduate and career officer who first served with the Gordon Highlanders before moving to the Intelligence Corps. Kerr had learned the ropes of counter-insurgency in Northern Ireland as a Det member of 14th Intelligence, the Province's main counter-intelligence squad. He was a senior instructor with the Special Intelligence Wing between 1985 and '86 before moving to command the Force Research Unit.

Lieutenant Colonel Kerr commanded the Force Research Unit

from 1987 to 1991; 1991 being the year that John Stevens was appointed to head an inquiry into possible collusion between British Intelligence and Loyalist paramilitaries. He was then promoted to the rank of Brigadier and posted to Beijing as British military attaché, many believing that British Military Intelligence thought it might be judicious to move him as far away as possible from the heat of the Stevens Inquiry. Ten years later, and while the Stevens team was still hard at work in Northern Ireland, the Ministry of Defence announced that it had no intention of launching an inquiry into Kerr and his role as FRU commander following information that the Stevens Inquiry team wanted to interview him.

During his four years as the FRU's commander, Kerr was known for his gung-ho, aggressive style of executing the war against terrorism, exactly the type of officer Mrs Thatcher was keen to promote and support in her determination to take the war in Northern Ireland to the Provos and fight fire with fire. Handlers tell of Kerr playing a very active role in his position as CO, pushing his handlers hard to provide as much detailed intelligence in their reports as possible, sometimes more than they felt was warranted by the facts before them. Kerr also wanted action. He knew that with Steak Knife and Nelson in unique positions in their respective terrorist organisations he was in a position to provide first-class counter-insurgency intelligence not only to his senior officers but, more importantly, to the Prime Minister.

Kerr sensed that his time had come: the opportunity to prove himself at the highest level had arrived and he was determined to make the most of it, not only to boost his future career but also to win the accolades of Mrs Thatcher, a politician and leader he greatly admired.

But Nelson's handlers were becoming increasingly uncomfortable with the agent's non-stop interest in the Provos and Sinn Fein. The task they had set Nelson was to provide them with information about the goings-on inside the UDA. They wanted to know names, addresses, car registration numbers, phone numbers and family connections of senior UDA members, as well as UDA plans. The FRU repeatedly urged Nelson to provide names of UDA gunmen and bombers, of UDA operations, targets, as well as the more mundane intelligence concerning finance, security and administration within the organisation. With this information, the FRU would be able to keep an eye on the UDA hitmen, draw up plans to prevent killings taking place and thwart other UDA operations. But none of this information was forthcoming.

Under the leadership of Lieutenant Colonel Kerr, the FRU had invested a great deal of time and money in recruiting and running Nelson as an agent, and they had expected him to repay them with top-class intelligence. In fact, Nelson was providing little more than pork scratchings, and the information he did provide was often useless or out of date.

What FRU did not know was that in spring 1987 Nelson had told the UDA leadership that he was working as an agent for British Military Intelligence. He perhaps believed that by telling the UDA he would be in a much stronger and more influential position within the organisation because he had a link through which he could obtain invaluable information on possible targets for the UDA. After Nelson had informed the four-man UDA high command of his other role, they decided to 'turn' him and persuade him to use his position as a British spy to their advantage. It is not known whether Nelson was happy or reluctant to agree to work for the UDA as a double agent. Perhaps he had overcome his resentment about the attack on his wife and had rediscovered his earlier desire to become someone of real stature in the organisation. Nelson had always been a Loyalist. It could be said that it had been bred into him and it may well have been that he had decided to work as a double agent before agreeing to take the job of chief intelligence officer for the UDA. Whatever the case, Nelson's subsequent actions proved that his heart still lay with the Loyalists and the UDA not with the Force Research Unit and British

Intelligence. From that time on, the UDA's Operations Branch were, in effect, using the Force Research Unit via Brian Nelson to help them in their plans to target Provos and Sinn Fein leaders.

In the early summer of 1987, Nelson had begun asking his FRU handlers questions about Alex Maskey, one of Belfast's most well-known and well-respected Sinn Fein politicians. Maskey, a well-built man then aged 35 and married with a young family, was at the forefront of politics in west Belfast. He was no fool and, anticipating that he was likely to be targeted by Loyalist gunmen, he took sensible precautions in his everyday life. Whenever he left his house in the Andersonstown area of Belfast, for example, he would automatically check for under-car booby-traps (UCBTs). His home, a three-bedroomed house on a large estate, was guarded by infra-red lights at the front and rear and had a spy-hole in the front door. He would never open either the front or the back door until he was satisfied he knew the identity of the person visiting him, and he told his wife and children to be just as careful. In the cauldron of hatred between the two communities in the late 1980s, this was the only sensible way to behave, checking everything and trusting no one.

A few weeks later, Nelson informed his FRU handlers that the UDA were taking a close look at Alex Maskey and wondered whether they would be able to help with information about him. Apparently, the UDA were suspicious that Maskey was not simply a leading Sinn Fein politician but also a member of the Provisional IRA. Nelson's handlers produced Maskey's P-card along with up-to-date black-and-white photographs of the Sinn Fein councillor. His home address, his telephone number, his car and its registration number were also supplied. At that time, Nelson was also provided with a list of the politician's friends and other people with whom Maskey regularly mixed. Of course, many of those on the list were members of Sinn Fein but there were also the names of some Provos.

Armed with the valuable P-card details, Nelson set about

examining every detail of Maskey's life on the home computer which had been installed in his home by British Intelligence IT experts. Nelson knew at that time that it was likely that Alex Maskey would soon become a target for UDA gunmen, indeed a highly political and high-profile victim of their new terror campaign.

But the execution of a UDA plan to kill Alex Maskey was more difficult than anticipated and Brian Nelson returned to his FRU handlers for advice. The UDA solution was to try and discover a way of luring Maskey out of his home and then shooting him. But how?

The answer became obvious when the UDA discovered that most mornings Maskey was collected by a taxi from a west Belfast firm which the UDA were convinced only employed former Provos and Republican activists. Maskey felt they could be trusted and used them almost exclusively.

A plan was thrashed out. The only way to guarantee success was to win Maskey's immediate and absolute confidence while he was still in his home. The plan called for a car from a Republican area to be hijacked by the UDA and taken to a friendly Loyalist garage, where a specially constructed taxi sign – an exact replica of the original – could be fitted to the roof of the car. Two weeks later, the car, with the sign constructed and painted, was handed over to Nelson.

At 9.45 one morning in July 1987, the fake taxi parked directly outside Alex Maskey's home in full view of neighbours, pedestrians or, indeed, Maskey himself checking through the spy-hole in his front door. One UDA gunman stayed in the driver's seat while the other walked to the house and rang the bell.

'Taxi for you, Alex,' shouted the man when someone answered the bell and asked who was calling. But no one opened the front door.

'Give me a couple of minutes,' came the shouted reply. It was Alex Maskey's voice. Though he had not ordered a taxi that morning, the FRU's understanding of the man proved correct. They had been convinced that Maskey would trust the fact that a taxi from the firm he regularly used had turned up, which often occurred when he was needed to attend an urgent meeting.

Two minutes later, Maskey unlocked his front door and stepped out. In front of him stood the man he had believed was a friendly taxi driver. But this now-masked man was holding a gun. Before Maskey could react, the gunman opened fire at point-blank range, hitting him in the stomach with three shots. Maskey fell to the ground and his attacker turned and ran to the waiting car. The UDA gunmen drove away unhindered. But this was not surprising, as the Force Research Unit had put an exclusion zone in operation on the estate where Maskey lived, alerting the police and any army patrols to stay out of the area. The gunman's 'taxi' was found abandoned by the RUC later that day. There were no fingerprints and no sign of a gun.

Maskey was rushed by ambulance to the Royal Victoria Hospital, where surgeons operated immediately in a bid to save his life. It would be weeks before the Belfast councillor recovered and doctors proclaimed that he was fortunate to have survived the shooting.

The RUC Special Branch was called in to investigate the attack and, from their own intelligence as well as informants inside the UDA, they were convinced the UDA had carried out the shooting. They also came to the conclusion that Brian Nelson had been responsible for planning the attack, more than likely with advice from British Military Intelligence, which they knew had recruited Nelson earlier that year.

This seriously concerned the RUC Special Branch senior officers, as it revealed that Military Intelligence were becoming more closely involved with the UDA. Until that time, Special Branch had believed that the UDA was 'their' organisation and that no other intelligence outfit, particularly British Military Intelligence, should invade their territory. RUC Special Branch had been made aware some months earlier that the Force Research Unit had been set up to act as a rival intelligence agency to MI5 in Northern Ireland in a bid to pursue the war against the Provos with more vigour. As far as the RUC were concerned, however, the FRU were involved only in gathering intelligence and nothing more. And of course MI5 had worked closely with the RUC Special Branch for many years, the two agencies frequently passing intelligence from one to the other and both keeping an eye on the nefarious activities of the UDA and other Loyalist paramilitary organisations, despite the fact that the gunmen and bombers of the Provisional IRA were the Loyalists' prime target.

Despite their suspicions about the FRU's involvement, no one from the TCG, MI5, RUC Special Branch or the Northern Ireland Office asked the Force Research Unit, their handlers or its Commanding Officer, Colonel Gordon Kerr – or, indeed, anyone – any questions over the shooting of Alex Maskey. Even inside the FRU, no questions were asked. It was as though no one in the FRU had known anything about the shooting before it took place.

All handlers were called to a meeting at FRU headquarters and a senior officer addressed them, saying:

> You have all heard of the unprovoked attack on the Sinn Fein councillor Alex Maskey and you must have heard that the RUC Special Branch are making allegations that Military Intelligence could well have been involved in some way with the shooting. Now, of course, we all know that is not true and has nothing whatsoever to do with the Force Research Unit. As far as we know, this shooting was probably the responsibility of the UDA and this information has been passed to the RUC for further investigation. We have contacts within the UDA, but, unfortunately, we do not always know when they are planning an operation, nor do we know of the targeted person or the location where this might be carried out.

> However, we must all make sure in future that our contacts
> with the UDA provide us with more details of operations
> planned by the UDA so that the forces of law and order can
> move speedily to prevent any killings or injuries of any
> intended targets, including, of course, any Provo, Sinn Fein
> or Republican activists, members or sympathisers. We must
> do all in our power to stop these random killings.

There was no discussion following the charade of this statement
from the FRU senior officer, but a recording was made so that any
future investigation could see how the unit's officers had reacted to
the shooting of Maskey. This was a sign that senior officers of
British Military Intelligence were already thinking of the future, of
possible problems, investigations taking place, questions being
asked, statements being taken as to the FRU's role in the dirty war
unfolding on the streets of Belfast in which the intelligence agencies
were now taking a far more proactive role than ever before.

Such activities, of course, continued through the two years or so
that Brian Nelson was working closely with both the FRU and the
UDA, and with each passing month he became more confident,
more assertive and more demanding. It became obvious that the
hardliners of the UDA were putting pressure on Nelson to provide
ever more intelligence about possible targets, whether they were
Provo gunmen and bombers or innocent Catholics. The UDA
killing machine had become obsessed with winning the war. They
were taking the battle to the Republicans and wanted results.

As Nelson made more demands on his FRU handlers for
personal information about Provo and Sinn Fein personnel, he
finally took his handlers into his confidence. 'Don't you fellas
realise that together, working together, we can destroy the PIRA,
kill every single one of the bastards? We should start with the
leadership. Cut off its head and the rest will die like the snakes they
are.'

Provos, Republican activists, Sinn Fein members and ordinary

Catholics came into the frame. Indeed, in the years that Nelson was working, allegedly as an undercover spy for the FRU, he was engaged most of the time in gathering intelligence so that the UDA gunmen could target those they believed were their enemies. The only time Nelson did, in fact, give any useful intelligence to the FRU so that they could intervene and protect someone's life concerned details of the UDA plot to murder Gerry Adams.

In the summer of 1987, Brian Nelson asked for an urgent meeting with his handlers and within a few hours he was sitting in a safe house talking to two of them. Before they sat down, the excited Nelson blurted out, 'I've got great news for you. We're going to bump off Gerry Adams and his bodyguard.'

Remaining calm, though inwardly worried, one handler asked him whether the UDA had fixed a date, time and place for Adams' assassination or whether Adams was simply a possible future target.

Nelson told his handlers that the UDA plans were far advanced and that they hoped to take him out within the next 48 hours. This worried the FRU handlers.

'Where?' asked the handler, a slight note of anxiety in his voice.

Nelson explained that the UDA planned to hit Adams outside the Belfast Housing Executive offices in the centre of the city. Nelson added gleefully that nothing could or would go wrong because the assassination had been authorised and planned to the last degree.

In a casual voice, another handler asked who was actually going to shoot Adams. If the FRU was going to save Adams' life, it was vital they learned as much as possible about the UDA plans. The handler, of course, had realised immediately that the assassination of one of the Republicans' most senior leaders was something that would have to be agreed at the highest level of government and probably by the Prime Minister herself.

Nelson maintained that he did not know the names of the people who would carry out the killing, but he understood that three would be involved. But Nelson did confirm that he personally had carried out the recce of the location at which the shooting would take place and that he intended to carry out another recce the day before the planned shooting.

Nelson then explained in some detail the plan that had been devised to kill Adams. Speaking in an agitated, excited tone of voice, Nelson told his handlers that he had decided to place one UDA man in a car parked in the square outside the Housing Executive offices where Adams worked. Using his two-way radio, the UDA man would notify two other men when Adams arrived at the offices in his chauffeur-driven car. The two men who would carry out the killing would be waiting round the corner on a motorbike. As soon as the rider received the radio message, he would accelerate to the offices, arriving precisely 60 seconds later. He had been told to slow down so that his gunman on the pillion would be certain to hit Adams with a hail of bullets.

Nelson then looked from one to the other handler for approval of his plan and they told him to continue. He went on to tell them that Gerry Adams arrived between half past ten and eleven o'clock every Thursday morning to attend a housing meeting. He was nearly always driven in his Ford Granada, an armoured vehicle and ex-police chief's car. Nelson told them proudly that he had obtained the colour and the car's registration number, as well as the fact that Adams was only accompanied by one armed bodyguard.

With a note of triumph in his voice, Nelson concluded, 'It's all worked out. We are certain to get the bastard.'

The handlers wanted to know how Nelson could be so sure that Gerry Adams would arrive on the following Thursday. Nelson replied that he wasn't positive but the fact that Adams turned up at the same time on the same day virtually every week meant there was every probability that he would turn up on the coming Thursday. Cocksure of success, Nelson told them, 'If he doesn't arrive this week, we'll just postpone the attack for a week. One way or another, we'll nail him, don't you worry.'

The handler then changed tack, telling Nelson that this plan was a very serious matter and he should have told them about it weeks ago.

'It was only decided a couple of days ago,' replied Nelson. 'I've been busy since doing the recce and planning the operation.'

While one handler tried to prise more information about the plan from Nelson, discussing the weapons to be used, the other left the room and spoke to a senior officer in Military Intelligence. Within a matter of minutes, the decision was taken at Castlereagh to let Nelson go, allow him to complete his recce the next morning and ask him to report back to his handlers immediately if he was given the go-ahead for the attack or in the case that any changes were made to the plan he had outlined.

As soon as the handlers returned to Castlereagh, the TCG was assembled and informed of the murder plot. Officers were ordered to devise a suitable plan of action to prevent the killing. The TCG debated whether Gerry Adams should be informed that a plot to kill him had been uncovered by British Intelligence, but it was decided not to do so, primarily because the TCG were confident they could stop the attack taking place without arousing undue suspicion. They also believed that if Adams was informed that he had been targeted by the UDA he might well decide to make political capital out of the alleged plot. But everything possible would be done to prevent the attack and ensure his safety.

The Joint Irish Section was informed and officers from 14th Intelligence were dispatched to the square to stake out the area, remaining under cover at the scene for the next 48 hours. They were informed that Nelson was expected to recce the square the following day. He did so and this was reported back. It seemed to the TCG that this plan could indeed be genuine.

As requested, Nelson reported back to his handlers, telling them that the plan for the killing of Gerry Adams had been given the go-ahead by the most senior UDA officers. When asked for the names of the three-man UDA killer squad, Nelson shook his head, telling his handlers that he had no idea of their names because, he claimed, the UDA senior officers who authorised the killing didn't give him such information. Before he left, Nelson was told to keep out of the square during the morning of the assassination plot. He nodded in agreement.

At nine o'clock the next morning, the square and the area surrounding the Housing Executive offices were being patrolled by 12 armed E4A officers and men from the 14th Int., all in various disguises and all wearing civvies. A strong military and police presence was also in evidence for anyone to see. Around the immediate vicinity of the square, fully armed, uniformed British troops were out in force, as well as more than 50 RUC officers. The plan was to scare off the UDA gunmen before they even thought of approaching the offices where Adams was expected to arrive sometime after 10.30 a.m. The officers from E4A and 14th Int. were under orders to take out the UDA gunmen – killing them, if necessary – if the terrorists did manage to break through the military and police cordon and appeared to be in a position to assassinate the Sinn Fein president.

At exactly half past ten Gerry Adams, accompanied by his armed bodyguard, arrived at the offices of the Housing Executive in the back seat of his armoured Ford Granada, totally unaware of the reason for all the police and army presence. Two hours later, he left the offices and returned home. There was no incident.

When Nelson met his FRU handlers the next morning they asked him, 'What happened?'

'The hit squad went out as planned,' Nelson told them, 'but when they approached the area they found police and army swarming all over the fucking place. They decided to split up and return to base. It would have been far too risky to go ahead in those fucking circumstances.' He said that the same plan would be put into operation in two or three weeks' time.

Two weeks later, Nelson informed his FRU handlers that the plan to murder Gerry Adams was still on and would take place the following day at the arranged time and place. Once again, the TCG ordered the security services, the army and the RUC to flood the place with armed men.

This time, however, the UDA driver showed extraordinary courage in the face of such a large number of armed troops and police, driving the car to the exact pre-arranged spot and waiting patiently for Gerry Adams to arrive. This daring move caused alarm bells to ring at the TCG, at army headquarters and among the top brass of Military Intelligence, for they suddenly realised that Gerry Adams could be driving straight into a trap which could well end in his assassination.

Orders were flashed to the 14th Int. troops in the square to watch out for the arrival of Adams and the UDA motorbike. They were ordered to shoot to kill the motorbike's pillion passenger if the motorbike was moving towards Gerry Adams' car. Every soldier, security officer and RUC man in that square was on alert, waiting expectantly. But nothing happened. The motorbike never turned up and neither did Gerry Adams. As a result of the second debacle, the UDA chiefs decided the plan would never work because there were always too many security men around the offices. They dropped the plan.

As a direct result of the Stevens Inquiry, Nelson was arrested on charges of conspiracy to murder in 1990, but he refused to take the rap for targeting and murdering PIRA activists, claiming, rightly so, that he was only acting under orders from FRU handlers. Stevens agreed, convinced that British Military Intelligence was guilty of collusion, and tried to persuade the British legal authorities, including Sir Patrick Mayhew, then the Attorney-General, that FRU officers and handlers should be charged with certain serious offences pertaining to Nelson and be brought before the courts. But Stevens was overruled.

Lieutenant Colonel Gordon Kerr, then in command of the Force Research Unit, told the court during Nelson's trial in January 1992 that it was likely that the agent had saved the lives of some 30 people who had been targeted by the UDA for assassination. But there has never been the slightest piece of evidence put forward to substantiate that claim. Those FRU handlers who were in daily contact with Nelson have been unable to discover any lives that Nelson saved, other than that of Gerry Adams.

Many other statements were made to the Belfast Crown Court during Nelson's trial in the attempt to portray him as some kind of hero. It was claimed that Nelson had been a prolific provider of information and that the Military Intelligence unit had produced 730 reports concerning threats to 217 individuals as a result of Nelson's information; that large amounts of UDA intelligence material was passed from the UDA to Nelson's home; that army handlers helped Nelson move UDA documents to a new address; and that the army photocopied UDA documents for Nelson.

Lieutenant Colonel Kerr also told the court of the alleged reasons why Nelson had agreed to join the FRU:

> Nelson was motivated by team spirit and loyalty to the army. I have no doubt that it was not out of loyalty to the UDA. I have no doubt it was to make up for past misdemeanours, to save lives and to eventually bring down the terrorist organisation.

On Nelson's behalf, it was also stated in court that he had been of 'enormous service to the community' and that 'many lives had been saved as a result of his activities; that Nelson had not been loyal to the UDA but to the army'. It was also argued that, 'Nelson was a victim of the system, but his was a case that should be regarded as wholly exceptional.'

Lieutenant Colonel Kerr even went on to describe in graphic detail what apparently happened to Nelson when he was suspected by the UDA hierarchy of being an army informer:

> He was taken to a house on the outskirts of Lisburn. Three

times an electrified cattle-rod was applied to the back of his neck, throwing him in convulsions onto the floor. He was kicked, punched, beaten up and brutalised but was eventually released.

The story was not completely true, however. Nelson was indeed subjected to the cattle-rod treatment and beaten up but that torture and beating had nothing whatsoever to do with his work as an undercover army spy. He had, in fact, tried to rape the girlfriend of a UDA officer. The torture and the beating were his punishment.

Indeed, Nelson had been a highly successful and proficient agent for the UDA throughout his years working for the Force Research Unit. Throughout his time as a double agent, he had provided much high-class intelligence, including names, addresses and information about Provo gunmen and bombers, Sinn Fein members and ordinary Catholics who had nothing whatsoever to do with the Provisional IRA. Some of those people had been murdered by the UDA as a result of Nelson's information.

At the end of his trial, Nelson was sentenced to ten years in prison after pleading guilty to five counts of conspiracy to murder. To the media and the general public, it appeared that justice had been done; that the rogue UDA intelligence officer had been punished for attempting to murder various people.

In reality, however, that was far from the truth. Before the case came to court, a deal had been struck between British Military Intelligence, the RUC, the Director of Public Prosecutions and an army of lawyers. Throughout the pre-trial deliberations, Nelson had always pleaded innocent to all the charges thrown at him, claiming that he was working for British Military Intelligence during the entire period. He refused to accept that he had ever done anything wrong in defending Northern Ireland from the Provo gunmen and bombers. He also refused to accept that he should face charges when Military Intelligence personnel were being let off the hook despite advising, encouraging and providing vital intelligence to him which enabled the UDA to carry out their attacks. Of course, Nelson was speaking the truth, but no one wanted to listen.

The Establishment, from the Prime Minister down, including MI5, British Military Intelligence and the RUC, needed a convenient scalp at that time, someone who could be blamed for all the misdemeanours that had taken place in Northern Ireland, including killings and shootings. Brian Nelson had been in the wrong job in the wrong place at the wrong time. The powers that be had decided Nelson was to be thrown to the wolves. And so he was.

But British Intelligence did provide a handsome sweetener for Nelson to look forward to as he sat in jail waiting for his release. In return for doing a maximum of ten years behind bars, Nelson was told that after completing his sentence he was to be provided with a new identity, relocation to any country in the world that would take him, £100,000 towards the cost of a new home and a lump sum in excess of £75,000. In return, Nelson agreed never to relate his experiences and never to write a book about his relationship with the UDA and British Military Intelligence.

As it turned out, Nelson served only some two more years' jail before being released. On his early release in 1994, he decided that he did not want to move overseas and a house was purchased for him in Worcestershire. His wife Jean had left him while he was in jail, their marriage at an end, and she took the four children and settled in northern England with a former handler of the Force Research Unit.

But there was to be another dramatic twist in the story of double agent Brian Nelson. In the spring of 2003, a short surprise announcement was issued by the Ministry of Defence to the effect that Brian Nelson had suddenly died 'from a brain haemorrhage'. He was just 54. Since then, no other information has been forthcoming despite the fact that he had been monitored on a weekly basis by an MI5 agent whose job it was to keep a constant and regular check on his welfare. This was no special privilege for the former double agent, for MI5 makes the same regular checks on a number of men and women living secret lives outside Northern Ireland because of the potential risk to them from former Provo and Real IRA terrorists.

To many sceptics in Northern Ireland's intelligence fraternity, it seemed odd that Brian Nelson should have died just two weeks before the publication of Sir John Stevens' report into alleged collusion between security service force members and Loyalist terrorists in Northern Ireland. At the heart of the Stevens Inquiry had, of course, been the murder of Patrick Finucane in February 1989, when Brian Nelson was at the height of his activity as a double agent. FRU handlers had been asked repeatedly by Nelson, on behalf of his UDA commanders, to find out as much information as possible about the solicitor's lifestyle and daily schedule. Nelson had left little doubt that the UDA were planning to target and kill Finucane.

On a number of occasions when Nelson had sought assistance and information about Finucane, the Force Research Unit had done all in its power to protect the solicitor, in the same way as they had saved the life of Gerry Adams some two years earlier. Each time the UDA came up with a new plan of attack to target and assassinate Finucane, the FRU handlers would find out from Nelson the time, date and plan of attack so that they could thwart the attempt. And each time they succeeded in doing so by swamping the areas with army and armed uniformed RUC officers.

Brian Nelson had been a focal point of the Stevens investigation, one of the few people Stevens believed knew the true story behind the solicitor's death. Importantly, the demands by Brian Nelson of his handlers to be provided with information on Finucane's whereabouts and his admission that the UDA wanted to kill Finucane placed him at the centre of the conspiracy to kill the lawyer. In fact, however, Nelson was not directly involved in

Finucane's murder. He may have been able to provide information to any public inquiry, long demanded by Finucane's family and supported in 2003 by Canadian judge Peter Corey, but his evidence would only have been circumstantial concerning the actual killing. However, Nelson's evidence in a public inquiry into alleged collusion would have been devastating, proof indeed that such collusion had been going on for years. With Nelson now out of the way, or dead, proving security collusion in a court of law would be extremely difficult, if not impossible.

But there is one question remaining: is Brian Nelson dead?

The Ministry of Defence did not give any details about Nelson's death. In the immediate aftermath of the news it appeared strange that there had been no need for either an inquest or even an autopsy. No details of a funeral, cremation or burial could apparently be found. Then, in April 2003, the *Belfast Telegraph* declared that they had solved the mystery, claiming that in fact the former agent had died in Cardiff, where he had apparently been living since the mid-1990s under the name of Brian Thompson. The paper also obtained a copy of a death certificate for Brian Thompson, which stated that he had died of lung cancer, from which he had been suffering from some time. They claimed that this explained the lack of an inquest, as his death was registered by a doctor who was caring for Thompson at the time.

There are former FRU handlers and RUC Special Branch officers who are, however, still doubtful that Nelson is dead. There had been no rumours, no hint within the intelligence services of Northern Ireland that Nelson had been ill or had been suffering from any illness during the previous weeks or months. If he had indeed been suffering from cancer, it was certainly not common knowledge among those who had previously worked with him. His former handlers all knew that Nelson was under the care and protection of MI5 from the moment he left jail. They knew he had been moved to Worcestershire, not Wales, given a new identity (not Brian Thompson as far as they were aware) and set up in a safe house and yet none of them had heard the faintest rumour that he was ill or in poor health. Of course, a brain haemorrhage can be, and often is, extremely sudden, dramatic and final, but not all that likely in someone who is apparently in good health. Intelligence officers have pointed out that giving the cause of death as a brain haemorrhage is always a perfect way to announce someone's death because it can be so sudden and unexpected.

Some handlers believe that Nelson has, more than likely, been spirited abroad by MI5, out of harm's way, so that Sir John Stevens' third report into collusion would be published with no Brian Nelson to comment, deny or give evidence about the findings. And, importantly, with no Brian Nelson to give evidence in any future trial, the Crown Prosecution Service would find itself in a difficult if not impossible situation finding witnesses who would be able to bring satisfactory evidence against those whom Sir John Stevens might have targeted for possible prosecution on a variety of charges concerning collusion.

In September 2003, the widow of Gerard Slane, who was shot dead at his home in Waterville Street, off the Falls Road, in September 1988, demanded to know whether the man convicted of conspiring to murder her husband was indeed dead. Gerard Slane had been targeted by the UDA, who suspected him of being a PIRA activist. British Military Intelligence had provided Brian Nelson with photographs of the man and his home address. The UDA gunmen had provided the killers and the weapons. It was a perfect example of the collusion that took place between the FRU, the UDA and the go-between, Brian Nelson. Mrs Slane said:

> Given that Nelson's death allegedly occurred in the week when John Stevens was to publish his findings on the policy of collusion between British state forces and Loyalist death squads, I was always extremely sceptical that he was a. dead at all; or b. that if he was dead, he had died of natural causes. The policy of collusion and the depths to which

Military Intelligence stoops have taught me that there is no such thing as coincidence or convenience.

Thus far I have not been allowed the truth as to why my husband, the father of my three children, was murdered and who was really behind it. However, I do know that Brian Nelson was a key player in his killing and I also know that the British Government struck a deal where he was protected from the application of law or justice in order to cover up the full extent and nature of collusion.

Mrs Slane went on to say that she would be writing to a number of British MPs asking them to table a question in the House of Commons on the issue. She said that she was calling on Tony Blair personally to state publicly whether Brian Nelson is alive or dead.

This author is unable to confirm whether Nelson is alive or dead. Those former FRU handlers who knew Nelson have been informed that he is indeed dead, but, in this extraordinary on-going web of intrigue and dirty dealings, of killings and murders that has been Northern Ireland's lot during the past generation, it would not be altogether surprising if this turned out to be yet another lie.

Chapter Six

THE SPECIAL BRANCH KILLING MACHINE

During the mid-1980s there was a deep feeling of anxiety, dejection and hopelessness that enveloped those on both sides of the religious divide who were not actively involved in the conflict that was tearing the Province apart. The vast majority of people living in Northern Ireland at the time only wanted an end to the non-stop violence and were exhausted by living in a constant state of fear. Mothers in particular were deeply affected by this anxiety neurosis and were desperate to ensure the safety of their children. Naturally, they looked to their menfolk to try and put an end to the killing and mayhem.

For the Republicans, the deaths of ten hunger strikers in 1981 had marked a turning point in the conflict. The anger amongst the Catholic population spilled out onto the streets once again and the IRA stepped up their strategy of indiscriminate bombings and attacks. This spurred the Loyalist paramilitaries into retaliation, as their leaders decided something had to be done to counter the Provisional IRA's campaign of terror. These Loyalists now believed that the forces of law and order, including the British Army, were incapable of protecting their families, so they decided to take the law into their own hands.

In 1985, the situation took a turn for the worse when word of a planned Anglo-Irish Agreement was leaked from the talks being held in London and Dublin, infuriating the Loyalists who, understandably, feared they were about to be sold out. The signing of the agreement in Hillsborough Castle in November 1985 had a dramatic and instant effect. The Protestants reacted with rage and a sense of betrayal, and even the most moderate rejected it out of hand. Sinn Fein, the IRA and most Republicans also rejected the agreement because it fell far short of their aspirations and, importantly, appeared to threaten their objective of total Irish unity.

Protestant anger showed itself eight days later at a massive Loyalist rally in the centre of Belfast. The placards bore the sign 'Ulster Says NO' and the speeches calling for an end to the 'shameful' agreement were greeted with roars of support. The scene was set for a ferocious Loyalist backlash – aimed at the innocent Catholic civilians of Belfast.

It is accepted that these sectarian killers were responding to the sickening violence perpetrated against the Protestant majority by the Provos, which included the immoral and shameful bombing of town centres and shopping arcades in which innocent men, women and children were killed.

A primary target of attacks in Belfast in particular was vulnerable taxi drivers, both Protestant and Catholic, who found themselves at the epicentre of the violence. They were easy targets, victims who unwittingly drove themselves to their own executions while carrying out their everyday jobs. No Belfast taxi driver felt entirely safe during those difficult days. Each and every time they went out in answer to a call, particularly during the hours of darkness, they knew their lives were at risk. It is a wonder that so many drivers were prepared to continue their work, answering calls from total strangers. But jobs were hard to come by in Belfast and money was scarce. Most taxi drivers felt it was a risk they had to take in order to feed, clothe and provide for their families.

It was known by the security and intelligence services that some of those men given jobs by taxi firms operating primarily in the Catholic districts of the city were former members of the Provisional IRA. Some had served time in jail for serious offences and some were still active Provos, members of the active service units responsible for killings, bombings and shootings. Two taxi firms in particular had attracted the attention of both the RUC Special Branch and the Force Research Unit, and the conclusion had been reached that these two firms were often used to move Provo activists around the city and, on occasions, transported Provo weapons and ammunition from place to place.

Some hardline Loyalists certainly shared this view and decided to take action. Sources have confirmed to this author that the Loyalists were supported in that decision by officers of the RUC Special Branch, who agreed to assist them.

In July 1986, two Roman Catholic men were shot dead in Belfast by person or persons unknown, and days later a third, Martin Duffy, a 28-year-old fireman and part-time taxi driver, was shot and killed when he went to collect a fare at Chichester Park Central, off the Antrim Road. Mr Duffy, a married man with three young children, lived in Manor Street, the scene of intense sectarian fighting during the previous ten days.

Martin Duffy's elder brother John explained:

> The firm received a call to send a taxi to Chichester Park Central and my brother was one of three drivers ready to collect a fare. He was unfortunately first on the list. Martin was just a poor unfortunate. There was no way they could have set him up in particular because those that killed him never knew which driver was going to be sent out that night.
>
> The thugs who killed him, when they heard on the news

bulletins that he was from Manor Park, decided to make false claims against him that he was a Republican. He wasn't a Republican and never had been.

It was not the first time that Martin Duffy had been targeted. 'Big Marty', as he was known in the fire service where he worked full-time, had survived an axe attack by a sectarian murder squad eight years before. On that occasion he had been lucky, escaping with a head wound that needed 16 stitches.

Following so closely as it did two other cold-blooded murders of Catholics, Martin Duffy's shooting in broad daylight kick-started law-abiding senior RUC officers into action, and a special squad of detectives was set up in north Belfast dedicated to tracking down sectarian killers. It was assumed by detectives at the time that a small band of hardline Loyalists was probably responsible for these killings.

One such Loyalist paramilitary organisation, the Protestant Action Force, a cover name used by the UVF, immediately claimed responsibility for Mr Duffy's death; they had also claimed the shootings of the other two Catholic men in the same district in the previous ten days.

There were, of course, a majority of Protestant politicians totally opposed to such killings but there were also many who accepted them and some who secretly supported the killings. One politician who spoke out against the killings was Ken Maginnis, the Ulster Unionist security spokesman at that time. He declared that he was ashamed that Protestants should engage in such sectarian killings. 'It goes against the whole ethos of Protestantism and it cannot be excused. The majority of Protestants whom I represent wish these killings to stop.'

The Irish Republic's Foreign Affairs Minister Peter Barry also condemned Duffy's murder and expressed his concern about the physical security of Nationalists in north Belfast to the British Government, saying:

The violence which too often is part of the marching season has claimed yet another innocent and defenceless victim. The killing is the sixth to take place in north Belfast since the beginning of the year. I call on both communities to support the efforts of the police to provide protection for all the people. It is time for responsible men and women in both communities to reject once and for all those, who, by word or deed, seek to provoke confrontation and to spread sectarian hatred.

But there were some rogue members of the security services who, far from wanting to bring an end to such killings, were positively eager to assist Loyalist paramilitaries in carrying them out. Sources have confirmed that there were some officers from the RUC Special Branch who gave the green light to the outlawed Ulster Volunteer Force (UVF), using the Protestant Action Force as a flag of convenience, to target taxi drivers. The Special Branch had trusted informers in every single one of the Loyalist paramilitary organisations and it was through these connections that those Special Branch officers were able to orchestrate the killings.

After several apparently random killings of taxi drivers, the local SDLP councillor Brian Feeney, fearful of the whirlwind caused by aggressive speeches by a number of Loyalist politicians, commented, 'We are now reaping the terrible fruits of the violent speeches by Loyalist politicians. We are in the midst of the most evil campaign of sectarian murder since the dark days of the mid-1970s in north Belfast.' Little did Brian Feeney realise that the forces of law and order were actively assisting the Loyalist paramilitaries to kill men they had singled out for assassination.

In a leading article in 1986, the *Belfast Telegraph* wrote:

In the past, the RUC has been notably effective in tracking down the perpetrators of such sectarian murders. The special squad of detectives which has been set up to deal with the latest outbreak deserves the complete cooperation of everyone who values the basic principles of civilisation. Such gangs cannot survive for long without the tacit support of the people among whom they live.

Atrocities like those which have occurred in north Belfast do nothing to help the Unionist cause. They only serve to deepen the divisions in our community. The killings will be gladly seized upon by the IRA to justify its equally obnoxious campaign. Ulster has been through the terror of tit-for-tat murders before, which brought nothing but misery. Everyone in the community can play a part in ensuring this does not happen again.

But the killing didn't stop and neither did the treachery of the security forces.

On 15 August 1986, a 30-year-old bricklayer, Patrick Murray, from the Short Strand area of Belfast, was found lying in a pool of blood in an alleyway some 60 yards from the Falls Road with a bullet wound to the temple. His eyes were taped shut and his hands were tied behind his back. A blue plastic bag containing his clothes and other belongings was found beside his body. A chilling statement from the Belfast Brigade of the Provisionals named the dead man as Patrick Murray and claimed he was an informer:

> The Belfast Brigade was aware for some time that information concerning IRA operations and activities was being supplied to the Crown forces in recent months and a thorough investigation was initiated to discover who was responsible. After exhaustive enquiries, evidence was gathered which pinpointed IRA volunteer Paddy Murray. He was arrested and when confronted with the evidence of his treacherous activities Murray admitted his role as an informer.

The long-winded 1,000-word statement went on to claim that, as an IRA volunteer, Paddy Murray was aware of his right to be tried by a jury of his peers who could not pass a sentence of execution 'unless the evidence against him was substantial and proven'. Faced with his own admission plus 'corroborative evidence', the IRA said the jury had 'no alternative but to find him guilty of the charge of treachery'.

The IRA also declared that Murray had been working as an informer since an arrest in 1978, when the RUC blackmailed him by claiming to have a weapon with his fingerprints on it. They claimed that in an agreement to avoid imprisonment, Murray became an RUC informer. The IRA also alleged that, among his activities, Murray told the RUC about an explosives dump in Killough which led to the capture of several volunteers and the seizure of the explosives. They claimed that in July 1982 he had received £2,500 for passing information about another explosives dump in Springfield Avenue which the security forces blew up, causing widespread damage in the area in what they claimed was a deliberate attempt 'to discredit the IRA'.

In keeping with a policy adopted in 1985, the RUC made a statement saying they would neither confirm nor deny that Mr Murray had been an informer. They simply repeated their previous statement in which they said it was a fact that people shot dead by the Provisionals had not been informers. Mr Murray's family strongly denied that he had ever been involved with or given information to the RUC or the Special Branch.

As with all of these killings, the Provisional IRA had once again taken upon themselves the roles of prosecutor, judge, jury and executioner. But they never mentioned in their self-righteous statements that many of the executions of alleged informers followed hours and sometimes days of appalling, insufferable torture before the victim confessed. And it was ironic that though the IRA carried out such travesties of justice on a regular basis, they and their political supporters had the audacity to complain continually about the normal judicial process within the British system while denying anything like it to the men and women they tortured and murdered.

The IRA never revealed how they had discovered Patrick Murray was a tout working for the RUC Special Branch and the truth was that they themselves never did uncover a connection. Sources have confirmed that the IRA were given the information in a shameful act of treachery by the Special Branch. Allegedly, Patrick Murray had become a nuisance to the Special Branch, taking decisions himself, acting without the knowledge of his SB handlers and, apparently, putting the lives of other SB touts at risk.

The betrayal of touts by the RUC Special Branch continued over many years and the SB adopted the same insidious method of treachery in the majority of circumstances when they had reached the decision that they wanted to get rid of a tout. A system of codes was devised so that contact could be made with the security wing of the Provisional IRA, giving the identity of a tout who was working undercover for the Special Branch. Throughout most of the Troubles there was a coded system whereby the SB could contact the security wing of the IRA and vice versa. Such an arrangement in the madness of Northern Ireland's civil war suited both parties. The Special Branch got rid of a tout they no longer wanted without having to dirty their hands directly, preferring to let the Provos interrogate, torture and kill the victims. And the Provos were able to demonstrate to their members that they had their finger on the pulse. They claimed they would always find out if and when a Provo turned traitor, and a dead body with a bullet in the back of the head illustrated better than anything the penalty of betraying the cause.

There were apparently a variety of reasons why Special Branch officers wanted rid of such touts but these can be condensed into four main categories. The first was that they had ceased to trust the informer; the second that they suspected the tout had become a double agent working for the Provos against the SB; the third that he had become a nuisance, making constant demands, usually for more money; and the fourth that the SB feared he was simply unreliable and a possible loose cannon.

Within a month of Patrick Murray being 'executed' by the IRA as an informer, a message was received by the Newry police from a barman who was driving along a border road with his wife when they came across a body. They gave exact details of its whereabouts.

Understandably, the security forces took precautions before approaching the crime scene, as on some previous occasions such tip-offs had turned out to be a Provo device for enticing unsuspecting police officers and army personnel to a lonely spot and then killing them, either by shooting them or laying booby-traps. On this occasion, a thorough aerial search of the beauty spot was carried out, as officers looked for any signs that the prone body was a PIRA trap and checked whether the man's body had been booby-trapped. Spotter planes took high-resolution photographs of the body and the surrounding area before it was sealed off by the army, and the security forces moved in to take a closer look.

The body of a man, later identified as David McVeigh, a 41-year-old labourer and father of three from Lurgan, was found on the deserted narrow road 100 yards from the border. His head was still covered with a black plastic bag and bound with black tape with no perforations, meaning McVeigh must have suffocated before two high-velocity bullets were fired into his head.

Later, the IRA issued a statement saying that McVeigh had been executed because he had passed information to the RUC. They claimed that McVeigh had been a member of their organisation and had been leaking intelligence to the police for some four years. As was usual in such cases, the IRA claimed the man had been 'arrested' and, when confronted, admitted his role as an informer. That was usually taken to mean that the victim had been tortured, sometimes over a number of days, until he finally confessed to whatever the Provisional security team of interrogators demanded.

The IRA statement went on to claim McVeigh had made a 'statement of admission' in which he detailed his activities, which first began after he was arrested by police in connection with an explosion at Lurgan Golf Club in 1982. According to the PIRA, McVeigh met his RUC contacts once every three weeks, when he was paid just £20. He was also allegedly given money for holidays. The IRA also claimed that he was once given a £200 bonus for tips that led to discoveries of arms and explosives, as well as the arrests of suspected PIRA members. The fact that McVeigh, a labourer, had received such pathetic amounts of money from his Special Branch handlers shows what a low-grade informant he must have been, making the IRA's killing of him even more despicable.

As a matter of course, McVeigh's murder was immediately condemned by politicians and church leaders alike. Newry and Armagh MP Seamus Mallon said:

> Once again the IRA have shown their hypocrisy about injustices caused by Diplock Courts and supergrasses when they decide to terminate a life in front of a kangaroo court on the strength of gossip. I believe the people of Newry will no longer tolerate this kind of brutality. They have seen too often the type of Ireland the IRA are trying to create – united at the point of a gun, built upon suspicion and cemented through fear.

In their killing of David McVeigh, the Provisionals showed they were prepared to execute a member of a family that had proved its belief in and dedication to the IRA cause of a united Ireland. Two of David McVeigh's seven brothers, Paul and John, were serving life sentences for murder: John had been convicted of killing an RUC officer and Paul of the murder of a former UDR man. Both murders were allegedly carried out on behalf of the Provos in the early 1970s.

The killing of David McVeigh, like so many other killings by the IRA, was courageously condemned by the priest Father Brendan Murphy at McVeigh's funeral service held in Lurgan, a town in which most of the inhabitants were Catholic, the majority supportive of the Provisional IRA and many of whom were active members. He said:

> Death always brings sadness and stings, but when it comes in the context of sectarian or paramilitary violence we are all left shocked and stunned by its cruelty. There is only a sense of utter helplessness in the face of this savage barbarity which turns hearts of flesh into hearts of stone. Violence stains, defiles and disfigures the fair face of our land. It diminishes our manhood, reduces our status and represents us as uncivilised maniacs before the nations of the earth. Violence has reared its ugly head once again in our town and parish and in its wake has snuffed out a young life.
>
> In spite of what David McVeigh may or may not have done, our condemnation is total and absolute, and there can be no more powerful example than this incident of the violence that tears asunder the hearts of people, leaving them more frustrated and embittered.

The real reason behind McVeigh's murder was that he had outlived his usefulness as a source for the RUC Special Branch. He had not only become a nuisance to his handlers, with constant pleas for more money, but there was also concern within the Special Branch that he had become 'unreliable', a euphemism suggesting he might have become a double agent working for the Provos.

On 14 September 1986, an IRA active service unit infiltrated the staunchly Loyalist Ballysillan area of Belfast and shot dead John Bingham, a 33-year-old father of two who the IRA claimed was a leading officer of the Loyalist terror group, the UVF. Two gunmen burst into his house in Ballysillan Crescent in the early hours of the morning while Bingham, his wife, Dora, and their two children were asleep. Two members of the terror group ran upstairs and shot Bingham several times as he came to the top of the stairs to confront the gunmen. The killers escaped in a car which was later found abandoned.

John Bingham was a well-known Loyalist activist who had received a 20-year jail sentence in 1983 for conspiring to arm terrorists and for possession of arms and explosives. But his conviction had depended on the word of one man, a UVF supergrass called Joe Bennett, whose evidence was later deemed unsafe, leading the Court of Appeal to quash the convictions of Bingham and 13 other men implicated by Bennett. Bingham was released in December 1984.

At the time of his death, Mr Bingham was unemployed, but following his murder, the IRA claimed that John Bingham was in fact the UVF's operations officer who had organised the murder of at least five Catholics in north Belfast during the previous few months.

During the spring and summer of 1986, there had been a total of nine sectarian killings in north Belfast. Most of the victims were Catholics and some had links with the Provisionals. The spiral of killings began with the murder of Leo Scullion, 55, shot dead at Ligoniel Working Men's Club, followed by Martin Quinn, 34, of Bawnmore Park, Newtownabbey, shot dead in the bedroom of his home. The third killing was discovered when the badly beaten body of John O'Neill, 25, was found in the stream behind the Boys' Model Secondary School in north Belfast.

In May, Mrs Margaret Caulfield, a Protestant married to a Catholic, was shot dead in her bed in Kilcoole Gardens, Ballysillan, after two gunmen smashed their way into her home. A 20-year-old construction worker, Brian George Leonard of Ashfield Gardens, Fintona, was shot while he was working on a building site on the Shankill Road. He died several days later in hospital. There were two more sectarian murders in the area in July: the killing of 25-year-old Colm McCallan of Millview Court, Ligoniel, who was shot dead outside his home, and also that of Martin Duffy. Two other men were shot and killed in cold blood.

This escalation in the actions and violence of the Loyalist paramilitaries came to alarm Ulster Unionist politicians, who persuaded senior RUC officers to take action against the gunmen. Community leaders, politicians, church leaders and newspapers also joined in the demands for the police to root out the killer squads and bring them to justice. As a result, the RUC were forced to take action against the paramilitaries they knew were behind the spate of killings.

Before dawn on 18 September, armed police squads raided Loyalist clubs in north Belfast and more than a dozen private homes, and a total of eight men were arrested. They were all brought to police headquarters at Castlereagh, segregated into separate rooms and interrogated about various killings and shootings. But these arrests and interrogations did not put an end to the killings.

Immediately following John Bingham's murder, the IRA claimed that Ballysillan was the 'undisputed base' of an 'extremely' active UVF murder gang and that John Bingham was the man responsible for organising many of the killings. The IRA claimed that Bingham had been moving from house to house, staying only a few days in one place to make it impossible for the IRA to target him while he organised the killings of Catholics and Republicans. He had also spent time staying in a caravan on the County Down coast. But a few days before they struck, the IRA claimed Bingham had felt safe enough to return to his home and they had subsequently 'executed' him.

Alarmingly, the IRA statement went on:

It should be noted that whilst we have no desire to get involved in a sectarian war, we shall avail ourselves of every opportunity to remove from the face of the earth those who callously gun down and murder our people. We are satisfied that Bingham fell into this category as he had a long history of UVF membership. We would like to state that the IRA will not involve itself in the execution of ordinary Protestants but we reserve the right to take armed action against those who attempt to terrorise or intimidate our people into accepting British/Unionist rule in the Six Counties.

Such a sickening, sanctimonious statement, of course, amounted to a declaration of war against the Loyalist paramilitaries. And both the British Army and the RUC believed the IRA's statement was also directed at them, despite the fact it was their duty to protect the whole population of Northern Ireland.

Most politicians accepted that the murders in north Belfast during that year had all the appearances of a tit-for-tat campaign designed to stir up sectarian hatred, and they condemned the IRA's killing of John Bingham, describing it as 'foul and sectarian'.

His funeral was one of the most well attended in Loyalist circles, not only by many influential and well-known Unionist politicians but also by more than 1,000 ordinary Protestant mourners who lined the streets, many wearing Orange sashes. John Bingham had made all the necessary preparations for his own funeral and had given instructions that members of the outlawed Ulster Volunteer Force should be told to stay away from the graveside because they had refused to support his terror campaign against Roman Catholics.

Even at the time of John Bingham's murder, questions were raised in Loyalist circles about how the IRA had obtained knowledge of his exact whereabouts, when he had spent weeks constantly on the move from place to place. Somehow, it seemed,

PIRA had learned of his return home within a matter of days. It is accepted that such murders are often planned weeks in advance and rarely are such killings carried out on the spur of the moment. There are those in Loyalist circles who today believe that the IRA had been tipped off through a Special Branch tout.

What has not previously been revealed was that immediately prior to his murder the RUC Special Branch had asked the TCG to order an exclusion zone around the Ballysillan area to ensure that no RUC or army patrols entered the area from midnight until 2 a.m. on 14 September. Hundreds of such requests were made throughout the years of violence, particularly in and around Belfast, and it must be stated that only very, very rarely did such requests end with anyone being shot or killed.

But on this occasion someone *was* killed. John Bingham had, in fact, been working as an agent for MI5 and as an informer for the Special Branch. But during the months before his execution by the Provos, Bingham had been engaged in the killing of ordinary Catholics who had no known connection with the Provisional IRA. It appeared to MI5 and Special Branch officers that Bingham had all but taken leave of his senses and was indiscriminately killing innocent Catholics. The decision was taken by MI5 that Bingham had to be stopped and the Special Branch were given the task. The information and timing of Bingham's return home was handed to the Provos and they immediately organised and carried out the killing.

As many had expected, John Bingham's killing did not go unavenged. Within hours, there was a warning of a possible Loyalist retaliation and it was not long in coming. Within days of John Bingham's funeral, three masked gunmen seized a man and a woman as they were leaving the Holy Cross Catholic Church in the Ardoyne. The masked gang shot Raymond Mooney, a married man aged 33, and forced the woman to watch the execution. After the shooting, they told her they were from the Protestant Action Force and were carrying out the shooting in revenge for the IRA murder of John Bingham.

At Raymond Mooney's funeral, Bishop Cahal Daly hit out at the words and statements which, he said, had inflamed passions and created a climate for murder. He referred to speeches being made by politicians on both sides of the sectarian divide who, he maintained, by their words were responsible for stirring up passions which inevitably led to killings:

> It is deplorable, it is incredible, that the day before Raymond Mooney's death there was a call by a public figure for revenge. Political spokesmen may not have intended the consequences which follow from their speeches but they should have foreseen them. Those who have been making violent speeches over the past nine months must now be the first to speak and to act against violent men and violent organisations in this community.
>
> Sadly, it must be added that there are pulpits in this land of ours from which a weekly torrent of polluted propaganda is poured out against the Catholic Church. We must pray and work, Catholics and Protestants together, to show that such behaviour has no place in our understanding of Christianity.

Dr Daly's sermon also lashed out at the IRA and Sinn Fein when he described the IRA's murder of John Bingham as 'a grievous violation of the holy law of God. It was also a crime against the Catholic community because it was a provocation to retaliation against innocent Catholics.'

The year 1986 had been peppered by scores of deaths across the religious divide, with paramilitary organisations taking the law into their own hands and, seemingly, indiscriminately killing many men often with dubious connections, if any, to terrorist groups. There were many killings of totally innocent people and, once again, these were mainly men. Some killings were obviously errors in targeting or identity but by January 1987 there was a feeling in government circles that the Loyalist paramilitaries, fed up with the non-stop aggression and the shootings and bombings of the Provos, had come to the conclusion that the time had arrived to take the initiative and carry the war to the IRA. The next 12 months would reveal whether the Loyalists would succeed in placing intolerable pressure on their sworn enemies or whether they would buckle under demands from peaceful Unionists to cool both their rhetoric and their violent actions.

Chapter Seven

THE KILLINGS CONTINUE . . .

Many Catholics whose homes were in the Ardoyne region of north Belfast felt they were living in a ghetto surrounded by hostile Loyalists who hated them. Many were convinced that the 'Prods', as they referred to them, wanted them dead. Others certainly believed that the Protestant majority in north Belfast wanted to cause so much concern, fear and nervousness among the Catholic population that they would quit their homes and move to a friendly Nationalist area of the city, where they would be welcomed. Towards the end of the 1980s, murders, shootings and beatings of ordinary Catholics had become regular occurrences in the Ardoyne, and the local Catholic cemeteries were frequently filled with tearful, grieving and angry mourners attending the funerals of those killed by Loyalist paramilitary forces. It was an ugly time.

In contrast, Sunday, 30 March 1987, had been a day of happiness and celebration in the Marley household in Havana Gardens near the Shamrock Club in the Ardoyne, as the extended Marley family attended the local Catholic church for the christening of the newborn baby daughter of Laurence and Kathleen.

Three days later, Laurence Marley, forty-one, a father of six, was at home with his wife when there was a knock at the front door of their terraced house.

Later, police confirmed what happened:

> The gunmen knocked at the door around 9 p.m. and Mr Marley went to the door and peered through the pane of glass in the door checking to see who was calling at that hour. The two gunmen must have seen his face peering through the glass for they then opened fire. They shot out the glass with a single round and then emptied a magazine of a sub-machine gun weapon through the wooden door before running back to the car and escaping down the street. Mr Marley took the full force of the attack.
>
> Mrs Marley ran screaming into the street for help from neighbours shouting that her husband had been shot.

Speaking after his father's death, Laurence Marley's eldest son, also named Laurence, then 19, explained the climate in which the family had been living:

> My father lived in constant fear because so many Catholics living in the Ardoyne had been murdered. He always took precautions to guard against a possible attack from Loyalists. He put bolts and a chain on the front door and iron gates at the bottom of the stairs. He simply knew that one day someone was going to have a go at him. He also made a point of never opening the front door until certain of the identity of the person outside.

The noise of automatic fire, the screech of car tyres and the ferocious revving of a car engine brought many out onto Havana Gardens to see what had happened. And when they heard a woman's screams for help, they all feared the worst. This wasn't the first time they had heard the sound of gunfire in that part of the Ardoyne, for it also housed the Shamrock Club, a well-known and well-attended drinking and social club not only for ordinary Catholics and Republicans but also for Sinn Fein members, as well as Provisional IRA activists.

A next-door neighbour, Mr Hugh Faulkner, said later:

> I heard about 15 bursts of automatic fire. The killers must have tried to empty every bullet into him. Just a few minutes after the shooting, my daughter answered the phone in our house and she heard a really sick laugh and then the phone went dead. That was despicable, sickening. We and the RUC believe that was probably someone gloating over the poor man's death.

It was yet another doorstep assassination of a church-going Catholic in the Ardoyne. In this instance, Mr Marley had been jailed in 1973 after being convicted of blackmail and membership of the IRA. After being released, he was re-arrested and this time convicted of arms and explosives offences. In 1977, he was given another ten-year sentence. He had been released some fourteen months before he was killed.

At the time of the shooting, two armed RUC patrols less than three hundred yards from the scene of the attack had set up roadblocks to stop and check vehicles and drivers entering the area. Allegedly, however, the RUC patrol did not hear the noise of the volleys of automatic fire from the two gunmen's weapons nor, apparently, did they see the speeding getaway car. It was subsequently revealed that the RUC patrols had blocked two of the entrances and exits to Havana Gardens but, for some unknown reason, had left one unattended, making it easy for the gunmen to arrive and leave Havana Gardens without being stopped, questioned or even seen. Understandably, this led people to wonder why on earth the RUC would go to the trouble of securing the two main avenues into Havana Gardens and deliberately leave one unattended.

According to Special Branch sources, the reason, of course, was that the murder of Laurence Marley had in fact been organised by the RUC Special Branch, who had tipped off the UVF and provided Marley's exact address. The UVF had also been informed by the RUC, via one of their touts, the date and time when best to stage the shooting. The rest was left to the UVF's execution squad. The reason the Special Branch wanted rid of Laurence Marley was, allegedly, that he had renewed his close relationship with his former Provo activists and it was feared that he was planning more atrocities against Loyalists. The RUC Special Branch had taken the decision to end his life.

As the army and the RUC moved into the area around Mr Marley's home and cordoned off Havana Gardens, groups of youths vented their anger at yet another Catholic killing by hurling bricks and bottles at the security forces. But no one was injured.

Twenty-four hours later the UVF claimed responsibility for the murder of Laurence Marley. In a statement, the UVF said Mr Marley had been killed by an active service unit of four volunteers using an automatic shotgun and a Browning automatic pistol. 'Two of our volunteers stood guard while two others knocked his door and they were left with no choice but to open fire when he came to the door and started to walk away again.'

The UVF went on to allege that after being released from jail, Mr Marley had once again become involved with the IRA and that was what had cost him his life. The Marley family denied these accusations but in a brief statement issued through the Republican press centre, the IRA countered the family's statement, claiming, 'Laurence Marley was one of our volunteers. To his whole family circle we extend our heartfelt sympathy.'

The funeral of Laurence Marley finally took place at the third attempt some six days later than originally planned because of a row over paramilitary displays. A controversial new law had been passed in the House of Commons making the display of guns and paramilitary uniforms at funerals illegal. It had been forcefully rejected by the IRA, who demanded the right to bury their dead in whatever way they wished.

Hundreds of Catholics and Republicans, many of whom had never met Marley or known his family, turned out for his funeral and scuffles developed between police and mourners at the graveside. To show their defiance, despite a heavy police and army presence, an IRA firing party wearing traditional IRA black berets appeared from nowhere and fired three volleys of shots into the air as a tribute to the dead man's service to the Republican cause. In a statement, the IRA said, 'We pledge in future to honour our fallen comrades in this manner. We will not be deterred from or dictated to by Crown forces and other elements from paying this final tribute.'

The heavy RUC presence at the funeral, backed by units of the British Army, ended with the controversial arrest of ten men, including three Sinn Fein councillors, for taking part in what the prosecution claimed was an 'illegal march'. The members of the firing squad were smuggled away by the mourners and were not arrested. At the court hearing, Magistrate Chris Milner issued a stern warning that people who flouted the new law and took part in illegal marches, including funerals, could expect to receive stiff penalties, including custodial sentences. On this occasion, some of the men were fined between £60 and £70, while others were given conditional discharges. The RUC's saturation of this funeral in a bid to prevent a paramilitary display was criticised not only by Republicans and Catholics but also by the influential Roman Catholic Bishop Cahal Daly.

Dr Daly said that parish priests insisted on an undertaking from families of those about to be buried that there would be no flags, emblems, political banners or paramilitary displays in the church or its precincts, but he made it clear that the Church had no control over what happened on public roads or at cemeteries. The British Government countered that it would be the wish of the House of

Commons that the dead – from whichever quarter or community or faction – should be buried in peace and dignity without any paramilitary displays or provocative demonstrations.

Northern Ireland Secretary Tom King criticised paramilitaries who were prepared to 'use' even a dead man as a propaganda weapon, saying:

> To allow unimpeded paramilitary displays at funerals would be very serious indeed. The answer lies in a responsible attitude and a clear recognition that the law must be observed. If the law is not observed, and if such organisations do intend on every possible occasion to stage paramilitary displays, then inevitably it will require police action, and that will raise problems for the RUC.

Laurence Marley's funeral, which some likened to a pitched battle between police and mourners, was a low point in the relationship between ordinary Catholics and the RUC, creating deep feelings of animosity. A gathering of Laurence Marley's relatives and friends to mourn his passing had degenerated into a public brawl in front of the nation's television cameras.

Even after Mr Marley's funeral the row continued, with Sir John Hermon laying the blame for the trouble at the funeral squarely at the door of Sinn Fein. Sinn Fein countered by declaring that the only paramilitary display and show of strength at the cemetery that day had been the RUC's – 'staged for triumphalist reasons'.

But the row over funerals could not hide the fact that the murder of Laurence Marley had caused concern among MI5 senior officers in London, because they feared that the killing was not yet another mindless sectarian murder but one which may well have been encouraged, if not directed, by the RUC Special Branch. Ardoyne Sinn Fein councillor Gerard McGuigan, a friend of Mr Marley's, said that since being released from prison Mr Marley had led a quiet life with no active involvement in either Sinn Fein or the

Provisional IRA. 'I do know that he was living in fear at the time of his death, fear that Loyalist paramilitaries might target him; that his life was in danger simply because he had been convicted of offences connecting him with the IRA.'

Six months later, two Belfast men were accused of murdering Laurence Marley. But in June 1988 they were cleared of any involvement in his death because of lack of conclusive evidence. However, those same two men, and two others, received heavy jail sentences after pleading guilty to conspiring to murder another IRA man at his north Belfast home in September 1987.

While the IRA continued to rage against the RUC over the funeral of Laurence Marley, the Provisional IRA were more concerned with domestic matters: disposing of one of their own members, Charles McIlmurray, whom they accused of being a police informer.

His body was discovered in a maroon Peugeot 304 van at 10.30 p.m. on Sunday, 12 April 1987, at a service station just yards north of the south Armagh border at Killeen. Charles Joseph McIlmurray, 32, a taxi driver of Slemish Way in Andersonstown, west Belfast, was a married man with two children. He was found bound and gagged with a plastic bag over his head. He had been shot twice in the back of the head.

Within hours of his body being discovered, the IRA issued a statement claiming responsibility for his killing, alleging that he had been a 'police informer' and 'agent provocateur'. However, doubt was cast on this claim by a Catholic priest, Father Denis Faul of Dungannon, who maintained that McIlmurray had in fact been a wholly innocent man 'caught between two ruthless forces' – the Provisional IRA and the RUC Special Branch.

The IRA claimed McIlmurray, an IRA volunteer, had been recruited by the RUC Special Branch after being arrested by police for drunk driving. In a statement, the IRA alleged that McIlmurray was told in an interview that if he agreed to supply information on

Republicans the charge would be dropped. The IRA further claimed that they had McIlmurray under observation for some time and that his role had changed from police informer to agent provocateur when he agreed to a Special Branch suggestion that he move weapons and explosives.

Father Faul claimed that the IRA's statement was of no value, as it was based on an admission forced out of the murdered man by torture. He also revealed that Mr McIlmurrary had contacted him one week after being forced to work for the Special Branch, which was exactly one month before his murder. McIlmurray had told him that as a result he was now living in fear of both the IRA and the RUC. The wretched man was scared to death that if he didn't work for the Special Branch they might betray him to the IRA, and he was scared that if the IRA discovered he was working for the RUC they would execute him. He didn't know what to do.

Father Faul said that he had assured McIlmurray that he would personally take up his complaints with the Police Authority on his behalf and told McIlmurray to explain this to Sinn Fein. Father Faul was convinced that he would have been able to resolve the problem without any loss of life if only the IRA had let him do so. He said that he had found McIlmurray 'very fearful and agitated'.

The case of Charles McIlmurray caused major problems for both Sinn Fein/IRA and the RUC Special Branch. Indeed, even Sinn Fein President Gerry Adams was dragged into the argument in an effort to quell the rising tide of criticism from within the Catholic community. Decent, ordinary Catholics believed that the IRA had murdered McIlmurray unjustly and that their reasons for doing so were dishonest.

Gerry Adams, of course, backed the Provos, saying 'Mr McIlmurray, like anyone else in west Belfast, knows that the consequence for informing is death.' He refused to condemn the IRA murder and said, 'We have always said that if people in such a position came forward and tell us what has happened, they would be treated leniently.'

Gerry Adams, a former commander of the PIRA Belfast Brigade, claimed somewhat contentiously that he could not speak on behalf of the IRA but went on to say that had Mr McIlmurray come forward to the organisation he would have put the IRA 'on a hook'. He said that people should take the IRA 'at its word' and contact Sinn Fein, a priest or a solicitor and explain their predicament in such circumstances. But that, of course, was precisely what Mr McIlmurray had done by revealing all to Father Faul.

Indeed, Charles McIlmurray had gone further. Taking the priest's advice, he had contacted his local IRA chiefs and told them of his predicament. However, in their statement to the press the IRA made no mention of McIlmurray having approached them but stated that he had in fact been 'under observation', implying they had been aware for some time that he was a police informer. That suggestion was untrue. He had explained everything, confessed all to the IRA and, for his honesty, had been executed, killed in cold blood. That is why McIlmurray's murder caused such outrage in the Catholic community, for the truth eventually seeped out and the IRA were seen to have behaved contrary to their own code of ethics. Some in the Catholic community described the IRA's action as 'despicable' and 'reprehensible'.

McIlmurray's murder also caused problems for the Special Branch, who handled the vast majority of Republican touts, for they were seen to have all but forced the taxi driver to work as an undercover agent on their behalf or risk losing his licence, and, as a consequence, his job and his sole livelihood. Forcing a man to risk his life working for the RUC when he had no real wish to do so was seen as grossly unfair.

One of the most extraordinary series of killings which stretched from the early 1970s to the 1990s concerned the unfortunate McCartan family. Throughout the 30 years of the Troubles, no family in Northern Ireland suffered more than the McCartans of

Belfast's Ormeau Road, who buried twelve of their loved ones, at least nine of whom were brutally murdered by terrorists. Brothers, cousins, sisters and nephews were cut down in the prime of their lives by a terrorist bomb or bullet.

The McCartan family were renowned for always mixing freely with both Catholics and Protestants, and there was never confirmation that any members of the extended family were members of Sinn Fein, the Provos, INLA or any other Republican organisation. The catalogue of the family's pain and grief reads like a never-ending tragedy. It vividly reveals the horror of the killings in Northern Ireland and how one family was torn apart by a succession of appalling murders and deaths, all linked in their various ways to the Troubles.

The first of the McCartan family murders, and certainly the most horrific, occurred in October 1972, when James Patrick McCartan, 21, who was working as a forklift truck driver, was abducted by the UDA from a party being held in a Belfast hotel. The full horrific details of his torture and murder were only revealed in October 1973 at what became known as the 'romper room' trial, when a former SAS soldier, Albert Walker Baker, pleaded guilty to murdering five Catholics, taking part in eleven armed robberies, and twenty-four firearms charges.

It seems Baker had deserted from the SAS after a wild drinking spree and offered his SAS skills and services to the UDA. Baker and his gang of UDA volunteers would tour Republican areas of Belfast, pick up Catholics and take them to a room in an east Belfast pub nicknamed the 'romper room'. There, the victims were beaten and tortured before being mutilated and shot, their bodies dumped around the city. Baker later claimed that he carried out these atrocities because they fitted in with British Intelligence's overall plan to terrorise the Catholic community into turning their backs on the IRA.

The second death, in March 1973, was that of a first cousin of James Patrick, a man named David Glennon, 45, who worked as a security guard at the Royal Victoria Hospital. He disappeared from the hospital one day and his body was later found in the boot of a parked car. He had been shot in the head by unknown assassins and his killers were never identified.

Another cousin, John Whyte, 26, a laundry presser, was killed in a freak accident on New Year's Day 1974, when an IRA sniper's bullet intended for a passing army patrol killed him instantly. James McCartan's youngest brother Noel, 26, was also shot in the head as he walked with his sister along the Ormeau Road in March 1974. Once again, there appeared to be no reason for the shooting and the RUC put his killing down to a drive-by assassin, a Loyalist hitman who had no idea of McCartan's name, age or religion but shot him because the warped mind of the killer conjectured that any young man walking along the Ormeau Road was likely to be a Catholic.

One week later, the same sister's husband, John Hamilton, 46, was shot dead in his home in Spruce Street, Belfast, after gunmen broke into his home and opened fire when Hamilton came to see what all the noise and commotion was about. No explanation was ever given for his killing.

James McCartan's nephew Gary McCartan, aged only 17, was gunned down in the hallway of his home in the Ormeau Road area of Belfast in May 1987 as he was combing his hair in front of a mirror before going out to meet his 18-year-old fiancée, Joanne Lavelle, the mother of their three-month-old baby daughter, Katrina. They were planning their wedding and were due to be married in a few months. It seemed extraordinary that a teenage lad should have been singled out that particular night when widespread violence rocked both west and north Belfast. More than thirty vehicles, including three buses, were hijacked and burned when police and soldiers came under sustained attack from gunmen and petrol bombs, and many Republicans clashed with the RUC and the army in violent demonstrations. Indeed, 7 May 1987 was one of the worst nights of violence and mayhem in Belfast for many months and yet the only person to be killed was Gary McCartan, who was targeted at his home. Some were injured when their vehicles were hijacked, others were fortunate to escape with their lives, but throughout the entire night there was only one concerted attack on someone's home – and that was the home of young Gary McCartan.

Understandably, there were long-held suspicions in the McCartan family about the possible reasons why their family had been singled out over such a long period of time. Some members of the family were staunch Republicans and some were rumoured to be involved with the Provisional IRA. It can now be revealed that the RUC Special Branch kept a very close watch on the family, suspecting some family members of having strong ties not only with the Provos but also with other criminal elements within the Catholic community. Indeed, as more and more family members were targeted and killed, there was deep suspicion that the Special Branch was responsible for giving information about the McCartan family to Loyalist paramilitaries and then standing back to see what the consequences might be. Intelligence sources are convinced that some members of the McCartan family were deliberately targeted by Loyalist paramilitaries with the assistance of the RUC Special Branch.

In the late summer of 1987, however, the RUC Special Branch changed tack, allegedly worried by the rise in the number of random killings. In fact, pressure from politicians and MI5 was the principal reason for the change of heart. As a result, the SB exerted increasing pressure on their colleagues, friends, relations and touts in the Loyalist community, urging them to reveal the killers in their midst. In particular, there was condemnation of Loyalist killings of ordinary Catholics who were not involved in any way with paramilitary activities.

It seemed the RUC pressure paid off in double-quick time, for in September 1987 a string of murder charges were laid against young Loyalists whom the police alleged had been involved in carrying out sectarian killings of Catholics, but this success opened the Special Branch up to criticism for not bringing such pressure to bear sooner in an effort to stamp out the indiscriminate sectarian killings which produced fear and loathing among ordinary Catholics and a spirit of revenge in the Provo hardmen. It was argued that by not acting more promptly against the Loyalist killers, the Special Branch had helped to sustain the appalling cycle of tit-for-tat sectarian killings.

But the dark trauma of death continued to stalk the McCartan family. James McCartan's nephew, James Hamilton, 35, was savagely beaten unconscious with a hammer during a horrifying attack in his own home in Harrow Street, Belfast, by a gang of three men wielding rods and iron bars who broke into his house in May 1989. He died in hospital several weeks later. That attack was put down as a sectarian killing by vicious Loyalists wanting to murder any Catholic for no apparent reason. But there were others who believed James Hamilton had been singled out and that his murder had been carefully planned using information that had been given to the Loyalist paramilitary squad by a tout working for the Special Branch.

Another family member, Gerard McCartan, who is not officially listed as a victim of the Troubles, was in hospital suffering from a rare blood complaint when he awoke one morning to find a UDA pamphlet on his bed. He knew full well the family history of deaths and killings and, fearful that his life was in peril, Gerard immediately discharged himself from the hospital and took a taxi home. Doctors pleaded with Gerard to return to the hospital because his illness was life threatening, but he was too frightened that he would be murdered if he returned. Gerard died of his illness while living at home; his doctors later confirmed that if he had returned to hospital they would have been able to treat him.

During the wave of sectarian killings carried out by the Loyalist paramilitaries during the late 1980s, the Provisional IRA did not simply sit back and watch. Perhaps the IRA's most high-profile coup occurred in late December of 1987, when John McMichael, the Ulster Defence Association's political spokesman and their deputy leader, was killed outright after getting into his booby-trapped car which was parked in the driveway of his home in Lisburn, County Antrim. The car exploded in flames when Mr McMichael, who owned a bar in Lisburn, turned the ignition key as he was about to drive away to deliver Christmas turkeys to the families of Loyalist prisoners. He died on the way to hospital. The IRA stated that McMichael's death was an 'execution of a paramilitary combatant and leader'.

John McMichael, 39, had been expecting such an attack from the Provos as retaliation for the shooting of one of Sinn Fein's best-known and most respected leaders, Alex Maskey, in west Belfast in May of that year. As described earlier, Maskey had been fortunate to survive the attack. John McMichael had told senior officers in the UDA that he was expecting a similar attack against either him or the UDA leader Andy Tyrie. But seven months had elapsed and it is likely that McMichael had relaxed his guard a little.

In their statement claiming responsibility, the Provisional IRA said that McMichael had been a prominent member of the Ulster Freedom Fighters terror group, which, they alleged, was planning a bombing campaign in Dublin and other towns in the Twenty-six Counties. The IRA also claimed that McMichael had a long record of involvement in cross-border and sectarian attacks and they warned Nationalists to be on their guard, saying that the UVF and the UFF had amassed considerable stockpiles of explosives. The UDA responded to the killing, saying they would take whatever action was necessary against the IRA at a time of their own choosing.

The fact that the Provos referred to the suspected bombing campaign in their statement revealed that someone, or some group of people, had made them aware of McMichael's thinking at that time. It can now be revealed that at the time of his murder there were senior officers in the RUC Special Branch and MI5 who had been watching McMichael for some months and they were worried that he was becoming too powerful, too confident and too ambitious. They were fearful that McMichael might indeed attempt to carry out some of his outrageous plans, for example bombing Dublin. And that was something that neither MI5 nor the British Government would have encouraged, for they desperately wanted to keep the Dublin Government on-side in the British Government's continuing war against the Provos.

Both MI5 and Special Branch had come to the conclusion that McMichael was rapidly becoming a dangerous Loyalist, a ruthless and charismatic leader who was attracting greater numbers to the UFF and the UDA mainly because of his hard-headed approach to the war against the Provos. He had also stated that the UDA was preparing for a 'head-on' collision between Catholics and Protestants and predicted this would occur within the next five years.

However, while McMichael's hardline commitment to the Loyalist cause was never in doubt, he was also probably their foremost political thinker. To some politicians in Northern Ireland, Dublin and London, McMichael was seen as 'the thinking man's terrorist'. He had been the main architect of the major Loyalist political document 'Common Sense', launched in 1987, which aroused great interest in politicians in mainland Britain, Northern Ireland and the Republic because of its emphasis on devolved government on a partnership basis. The document reflected a growing awareness at grassroots level in Loyalism that Unionist politicians should become involved in dialogue and attempt to work out a political solution with constitutional Nationalists.

According to security sources, however, McMichael had other irons in the fire that the RUC didn't like. They suspected that McMichael was involved in ongoing criminal activities, particularly protectionism, extorting money from Protestant firms and companies in an effort to secure a ready supply of funds to the UFF cause. The UFF needed money for arms, ammunition, training and to pay volunteers and, importantly, touts.

The killing of John McMichael was a major blow to the UDA's political ambitions, and there were those who questioned whether it was as straightforward as another attack by the IRA. UDA commander Andy Tyrie, a close friend and political soulmate of John McMichael, reported after the killing that his friend had been aware that he was being followed by Republican groups for some months and he found it strange that the security forces had offered him no form of protection. Only 48 hours before his death, John McMichael had commented that the area around his home had been 'crawling with police', believing the RUC must have received information about a possible attack on him. He had found reassurance in the fact that the RUC were in the area in considerable numbers.

Low Road in Lisburn, where John McMichael lived, was on a housing estate and a close-knit almost exclusively Protestant area where any strangers would have been quickly spotted and the police called to investigate. His neighbours were also well aware that John McMichael was a prime IRA target who had lived away from his home for months at a time for fear of such an attack. And yet, the people who laid that booby-trap must have been strangers to the area and they must have taken some time to lay and prime the booby-trap under McMichael's car sometime after it got dark around 5 p.m.

Intelligence sources have told this author that the RUC had been withdrawn from the estate earlier that evening and there were no police to be seen. The way was clear for the IRA bombers to infiltrate Low Road and make their way unhindered and unnoticed in the darkness to McMichael's house to lay their booby-trap. It can now be revealed that the Special Branch had, in fact, arranged for one of their touts to inform the Provos of the time and the date when John McMichael would be at home. The Special Branch had also provided the exact address.

After his killing, the circumstances surrounding McMichael's death were examined and debated. Some political analysts believed the IRA's murder of a high-profile hardline Loyalist politician like John McMichael was an attempt to recover some of its credibility in the wake of the Enniskillen Remembrance Day atrocity the previous month, one of the IRA's worst-ever propaganda disasters.

There were other theories for the murder. In the local Northern Ireland elections in the spring of 1987, Sinn Fein had suffered serious setbacks as a result of their unsuccessful election campaign based on the slogan 'the Armalite and the ballot box', first mentioned as a strategy in 1981 at a Sinn Fein Ard Fheis. The theorists maintained the IRA had therefore abandoned that strategy in favour of a policy of confrontation and provocation. The killing of McMichael was seen as the first step.

During that Christmas and New Year holiday, many in Northern Ireland had waited with bated breath to see what the New Year would bring. There was not too much enjoyment and merriment, for many people on both sides of the divide feared a dramatic upsurge of attacks, killings and bombings would quickly follow.

Chapter Eight

DEATH ON THE ROCK — THE REAL STORY

Despite thousands of words written in newspapers, magazines and books about the killing of three members of a Provo active service unit in Gibraltar in March 1988, the full story has never before been revealed. Mairead Farrell, Danny McCann and Sean Savage were specially selected for this high-profile bomb attack in Gibraltar, which was intended to maim and slaughter scores of innocent tourists, as well as soldiers mounting the ceremonial guard that day. They had never worked together before as members of an ASU but this attack was intended to be an IRA spectacular. A great deal of thought and planning went into the operation over a period of some six months.

Little did they, or the Provo planners, know, however, that their entire operation to bomb Gibraltar was known about from the time the plans were drawn up. British Intelligence was aware of the IRA's intention to plant a car bomb in Gibraltar weeks before the three bombers ever set out from Belfast on their murderous trip to the sun. A strategy was devised to stop the bombing and kill the three ASU members in order to demonstrate to the IRA leadership, the British people and political leaders in Europe that the Government was no longer simply at the mercy of IRA terrorists. They wanted to show the world that they now possessed the intelligence capability to intercept planned terrorist actions and would be ruthless when dealing with IRA terrorists bent on killing innocent people. The public 'execution' of the three members of the ASU sent to bomb Gibraltar demonstrated their commitment to use any means necessary to counter the threat posed by the Provos and they planned the operation so that the 'executions' took place in full view of tourists and sightseers.

The British Government badly needed a success. The previous winter the Provos had committed one of the most horrific atrocities of the 30 years of the Troubles. On 8 November 1987, a bomb exploded without warning in the St Michael's Reading Room in Belmore Street in Enniskillen, County Fermanagh, as men, women and children gathered outside the building prior to the annual Remembrance Day service at the town's war memorial. Eleven people were killed, among them six pensioners and a nurse, and sixty-three were injured.

The IRA had also been highly successful in Europe, causing severe embarrassment to the Thatcher Government. The Provos had set up a number of ASUs in West Germany, Holland and Belgium, and MI6 were having grave problems in tracking them down, despite help from intelligence services across Europe.

In March 1987, the IRA carried out a car bomb attack on the headquarters of the British Army of the Rhine at Rheindahlen in West Germany, injuring some 30 people in the blast. It was the first of some 20 attacks in West Germany and Holland against British service personnel over the next three years. Such attacks on the European continent were very bad publicity for Britain, the Government and the British tourist industry.

Carrying their war to Europe, however, brought the IRA into direct confrontation with Europe's international intelligence agencies and networks, which were increasingly cooperating with each other in a bid to challenge and defeat not only the IRA but also other terrorist organisations fighting the established governments in France, Spain, Germany and Italy in particular. Of course, the Basque separatist movement ETA is often considered to be mainland Europe's equivalent to the IRA but there were also other movements which the intelligence agencies were watching. Fearful that the IRA might escalate their attacks, Germany, France, Holland, Denmark, Sweden, Italy, Spain and Austria agreed to on-pass to the British intelligence services any information they came across concerning possible IRA activity in their countries.

It was as a result of such intelligence cooperation that the French seized tons of explosives, ammunition and weapons destined for the IRA on board the ship MV *Eksund* off the French coast in October 1987. But other shiploads of weapons and explosives did reach their destinations and, as a result, the IRA built up substantial arms, explosives and ammunition dumps in southern Ireland.

The British security forces also had some success in 1987. The most dramatic of these actions occurred on the evening of Friday, 8 May 1987, in the tiny village of Loughgall, a picturesque spot on the back road between Portadown and Armagh. From the IRA's viewpoint, Loughgall was an ideal target for an IRA bombing, as the village was well known as a founding centre of Orangemen and its 250 inhabitants were almost exclusively Protestant.

The Force Research Unit had been tipped off by Steak Knife that the Provos were planning a campaign of targeting police stations and security bases. The Provos' plan was to target as many small, isolated and vulnerable RUC stations as possible, forcing the authorities to close them down rather than risking the lives of the few RUC officers who operated them. This would ensure that vast swathes of the country in Northern Ireland were left with no police stations, meaning that the Provo ASUs could then roam the country with virtually no hindrance and with very little chance of their movements becoming known.

The insignificant four-man Loughgall RUC station was in fact the twelfth to be targeted that year and the seventh in a two-week spell. Most of the earlier attacks had been made with home-made mortars and though the police stations and army bases had been hit, no one had been killed or injured and little structural damage had occurred.

Unfortunately, while the FRU had learned that the IRA were intending to send a large squad of well-armed gunmen to Loughgall, they had been unable to determine the exact time and date of the proposed IRA attack and the SAS had been put on stand-by to move into place around the Loughgall station for an indefinite stake-out. In fact, by luck more than good judgement, the very day after the 20 well-armed SAS men had moved into position in the fields opposite the RUC station, an observation post on the road some distance from the village radioed that a digger was rumbling down the road towards the target.

As the FRU had been informed that the Provo ASU intended to destroy the single-storey building with one massive bomb, putting it totally out of action, orders had been given to vacate the place, meaning there was no immediate risk to anyone's life. SAS detachments sent to Northern Ireland were frequently frustrated that they were not permitted to take a more active part in tackling Provo gunmen and this seemed a golden opportunity to have a crack at the enemy.

Silently, the SAS men, lying low in heavy camouflage behind the hedgerow across the road from the deserted station, cocked their weapons – and waited. Shortly after 7 p.m., a blue Toyota van made its way through the village, turned and came back past the RUC station. Some 15 minutes later, the SAS troops saw the yellow digger trundling towards them with a driver and two men in boiler suits standing on either side of the vehicle, their faces hidden by masks. They were carrying AK-47s. Twenty yards or so behind the digger, the blue Toyota van, stolen from a street in Dungannon earlier that day, was being driven at the same speed as the slow-moving digger.

As the two vehicles approached the station, the Toyota van passed the digger and came to a halt smack outside the police station, only yards from where some SAS men were lying. The driver of the digger slowed almost to a halt, then turned the vehicle towards the entrance of the deserted station and, with the three men still on board, smashed through the barbed-wire perimeter fence and trundled towards the white façade of the building. Seconds before the digger crashed into the police station, the three men jumped off and ran back towards the road through the gap in the fence. As they ran out, the rear door of the Toyota was thrown open and half a dozen men, also dressed in dark boiler suits and wearing masks, jumped out. All were armed, some with AK-47s, others with handguns.

No warning was shouted to the Provo gunmen, no effort was made to arrest them. Instead, the SAS opened fire, pouring hundreds of rounds at the men, determined to wipe out the entire IRA unit. Some took refuge behind the van and returned fire, but the majority, realising they had been caught in a ferocious ambush, simply ran for their lives.

Suddenly, the air was rent with the most enormous explosion and the entire roof of the RUC station was lifted into the air. Thousands of tiles and blocks of masonry were hurled high above the ground and some came crashing down amongst the Provos and the SAS troops. Shielded by the van, one or two IRA gunmen managed to get off a few rounds but they dared not leave the protection of the van for fear of being cut to ribbons. They also had no idea where the SAS troops were hidden, but they knew from the ferocious noise of the firing, and the number of rounds smashing into their van, that they were out-numbered and out-gunned. Finally, the gunmen decided to make a run for safety, but before those behind the van had taken more than a few steps, they were cut down with witheringly accurate fire. They were given no chance to surrender and not one escaped the SAS ambush. The SAS had fired over 1,000 rounds, the Provos had managed to get off only 100. Eight IRA men were killed and not a single SAS man received any injury. Incredibly, there were no demands from any quarter for a police or public inquiry into the killings.

The operation at Loughgall was a major coup for the intelligence services and a disaster for the Provisional IRA, resulting in the deaths of some of its most noted hardmen at a time when its political wing, Sinn Fein, was already suffering from a considerable drop in electoral support throughout the Province. Indeed, following the Loughgall massacre the Thatcher Government came to believe that they now had the Provos on the run. As a result of increased intelligence and a harder line being taken against the gunmen and bombers, the Provos' fighting strength had been seriously depleted by security force successes from around 1,000 in 1980 to less than 250, of whom only some 50 men were members of active service units, the remainder providing logistical support.

Despite these losses, however, the following year saw the level of violence escalate dramatically, to the extent that 1988 proved to be the worst year for army casualties, and was never to be equalled. During the month of March alone, there were 17 bomb attacks and 20 shooting incidents, and there was a real fear in political circles that the British Government had lost the initiative in their efforts to bring IRA terrorists to justice, lost control of the situation on the streets of Belfast and were in danger of losing the war against the organisation. That was a situation that Mrs Thatcher was not prepared to tolerate.

Following the Loughgall disaster, the IRA's ruling Army Council, spurred on by hardline elements from the Belfast Brigade, were hell-bent on revenge. They recognised that there was a need to boost flagging morale within the Republican movement and they fully realised that recruiting new young IRA members would be very difficult following such a massacre.

There was a long and serious debate: there was no immediately obvious easy target for a Provo ASU in Northern Ireland because the British intelligence services now appeared to be learning of IRA operations before actions were carried out. Fears of such leaks of planned IRA operations had a serious effect on the newly formed active service units because they were not so keen to endanger their lives and their freedom carrying out risky attacks. Since the Brighton bombing of 1984, the Army Council also recognised that security had been tightened up on the mainland and easy targets were difficult, if not impossible, to find. They therefore decided they had to concentrate on a major bombing attack on a British target in Europe, where security was not high and the risk of losing any more men was negligible.

Once this decision was made, Gibraltar seemed the ideal target. A garrison of some 1,500 British troops was permanently stationed there, and the Rock also accommodated a vital Government Communications Headquarters (GCHQ) and a NATO listening post which monitored radio traffic and the movement of Soviet naval forces through the straits which link the Mediterranean and the Atlantic. It was therefore an important strategic outpost and any attack on it would have a major impact on Britain, be highly embarrassing for the Thatcher Government and would hit the headlines around the world, raising the international profile of the IRA.

The IRA Army Council came to the conclusion that this was such an important task that they would send three experienced activists: Danny McCann, Sean Savage and, the most controversial selection, Mairead Farrell, the well-educated daughter of a middle-class Catholic family from west Belfast. Mairead, an attractive, well-spoken and intelligent girl, had joined the IRA at the age of 18. She took part in the bombing of a hotel in Dunmurry in 1976 and was sentenced to 14 years in jail, becoming the first female Republican to be imprisoned after terrorists lost their special category status. While in prison, she took part in a 'dirty protest' and in December 1980 went on a 19-day hunger strike. In 1986, she was released and thereafter had been studying politics and economics at Belfast's Queen's University.

The IRA plan was for a car-bomb attack on the troops changing the guard outside the Governor's residence, a ceremony carried out every Tuesday at 10.55 a.m. by the resident British infantry battalion in Gibraltar, in this instance the 1st Battalion of the Royal Anglian Regiment, which had just completed a tour of duty in Northern Ireland.

Following a tip-off from Steak Knife some five months before the planned attack, Savage and McCann were discovered in Malaga on Spain's Costa del Sol in November 1987 by a British agent working for the 14th Intelligence Company. He was ordered to stay in Malaga and await developments, and reported that arms and explosives had been cached there.

Thatcher took the decision to follow and not intercept the Provo ASU after she had received assurances from senior MI5 officers that if the operation was handled correctly and one or two SAS 'bricks' were flown to the Rock, there would be little or no threat to members of the public living in or visiting Gibraltar. Thus 'Operation Flavius' was born.

The arms and explosives for the attack had been purchased from the Palestine Liberation Organisation (PLO) on behalf of the Provisional IRA by ETA. The IRA paid £200,000 to ETA for the arms and assistance on this mission. Most of this money was passed to the PLO to help maintain production of their newspaper. For their part, ETA imported the arms and explosives into Spain and then moved them to what they believed was a safe and secret location in Malaga on Spain's Costa del Sol. ETA also stole the vehicles needed for the IRA mission, including the car that would contain the bomb, and they provided secure accommodation for the three Provo terrorists during their stay in Spain.

In November 1987, Savage and McCann, using the aliases of Robert Reilly and Brendan Coyne, were spotted at Madrid Airport and the Spanish authorities passed this piece of evidence to MI5. From that moment surveillance was increased by MI5, who sent agents to Madrid, Malaga and Gibraltar.

In January 1988, Belgian police hunting a gang of crooks involved in a series of major robberies discovered 110 lb of Semtex and other bomb-making equipment concealed in a Dutch-registered Renault 5 in a garage in Brussels. This piece of information was passed to police forces across Western Europe and the Dutch police were tasked with determining the ownership of the Renault. It seems that this piece of information related to another planned IRA attack in northern Europe which never took place.

Some weeks later, Savage and McCann travelled to San Sebastian and were given two weeks' training by ETA bomb-makers in assembling, fixing and preparing under-car booby-traps. Throughout that visit to San Sebastian, British Intelligence was assisted on the ground by members of Spain's secret intelligence service. In turn, they were receiving intelligence from one of their spies who had successfully infiltrated the Basque separatist movement. They were able to ascertain that an IRA operation was being planned but they had no further details.

At the end of February 1988, heightened movement among the terrorists had alerted MI5 to the possibility that the IRA attack was imminent. Word was received from 14th Int. agents in Dublin that Savage and McCann had been seen boarding a flight to Belfast, from where they travelled on to Spain. This news was flashed to MI5 headquarters in London and to the MI5 teams in Malaga and Gibraltar. Mairead Farrell was also sighted at Dublin Airport boarding a flight to Brussels. The Belgian police kept watch and reported that she had arrived and then taken a direct flight to Malaga. MI5 already had some dozen men in both Malaga and Gibraltar and an operations room had been set up in the Gibraltar Police Headquarters, from where they could monitor everything that was happening on the Rock. The ASU team briefly met up at a crowded Malaga Airport and then Mairead Farrell left the two men and was lost in the crowds. McCann and Savage were seen getting into an airport taxi.

On 2 March, the Joint Intelligence Committee in London alerted
the Joint Operations Centre at the Ministry of Defence, which in
turn gave orders for the deployment of a 22 SAS counter-terrorist
team from the squadron. The following day, two SAS four-man
bricks, accompanied by the squadron commander, two senior SAS
officers and an explosive ordnance disposal expert, flew to
Gibraltar, where they linked up with MI5 officers and the Gibraltar
Police Special Branch unit.

The two IRA men had been tracked to the Hotel Florida in
nearby Fuengirola but then the trail had gone cold. Seemingly, they
had just disappeared. Neither had checked into the Hotel Florida
but were seen arriving outside. These were desperate hours for
everyone involved in Operation Flavius, from Prime Minister
Thatcher down. It is understood that she was 'spitting blood' when
told that all three members of the Provo ASU had slipped through
the elaborate net which had taken weeks of diligent intelligence
organisation to prepare and had now disappeared into the
proverbial thin air.

Spanish police were requested to carry out a search of every
hotel in Fuengirola as a matter of urgency in a bid to find the two
men. In fact, they had picked up a car left for them by ETA and
driven to the resort of Torremolinos, where at midnight they
checked into the Hotel Residencia Escandinavia for two nights
under the names of Coyne and McArdle. The room had three beds
and, importantly, direct access to a street at the rear of the hotel.

It seems that Mairead Farrell had also escaped the watching MI5
and 14th Intelligence Company teams, as she arrived at the Hotel
Residencia Escandinavia the same day and stayed there that night,
leaving behind make-up and some women's clothing. She didn't
check in and was never seen by any of the hotel staff. This is not
so surprising, as ETA contacts were used to carry out such tasks as
checking into hotel rooms, hiring vehicles and sometimes driving
vehicles from point to point.

Fortunately, however, routine checking by Spanish police of car rental firms in Torremolinos the following day threw up the vital fact that a man fitting Savage's description had rented a white Renault 5, while Mairead Farrell made a similar booking for another vehicle with another rental firm in Marbella, some 40 miles nearer Gibraltar. But the pressure was still on those desperately searching for the three Provos, as a confirmed sighting had not been made since they arrived in Malaga some 36 hours earlier. There was a desperate fear that the ASU might abort their plans to bomb Gibraltar and leave a car bomb in the holiday resorts of Marbella or Torremolinos, both frequented by British tourists.

Sometime after the ASU team flew into Malaga, a red Ford Fiesta, rented from a car firm in Torremolinos by an unknown Irishman, was expertly packed with 140 lb of Semtex and driven to the basement of a multi-storey car park at Edificio Marbeland. In the early hours of 6 March, Savage, McCann and Farrell drove the 30 miles from Torremolinos to Marbella in a white Ford Fiesta and parked the vehicle in the basement car park right next to the red Ford Fiesta car bomb. It was during this drive to Marbella that the Provo ASU were sighted and from then on their movements were tracked every inch of the way to their Gibraltar destination.

There was a huge sigh of relief from everyone involved, from MI5, the 14th Int. and especially everyone in London who had been responsible for Operation Flavius. The order came back from London, 'It is of paramount importance these three people are kept under surveillance 24 hours a day.' As someone in the Gibraltar police headquarters quipped at the time, 'They're just covering their arses.'

As the Provos were driving towards Marbella, a 1 a.m. briefing was held in Gibraltar by the senior MI5 officer in command of Operation Flavius on the ground. Officers from the SAS, 14th Int., the Gibraltar Special Branch and others were called in and given a detailed analysis of the serious bomb threat. They were informed that the car bomb would most likely be set off via a radio-controlled device.

At this meeting, the SAS were briefed on the rules of engagement, the degree of force to be used and conditions under which the SAS men could open fire. However, what has never before been revealed is that the SAS team of three men were later told, 'Don't ask questions . . . Shoot to kill . . . take no chances. One of these three will be holding the radio-controlled device so make sure all three are taken out.'

Sometime around midday on 6 March, Savage, McCann and Mairead Farrell arrived in Gibraltar. As soon as the ASU team set foot on British territory, MI5 kept a close eye on them. MI5 agents, including a number of women, were used to carry out a close surveillance of the three terrorists. Those in command in Gibraltar and back in No. 10 Downing Street wanted to be 100 per cent certain they were tailing the right three people.

As it was March and the beginning of spring in sunny Gibraltar, there were a number of tourists and daytrippers on the Rock, which made it easy for the MI5 agents to masquerade as tourists. Sean Savage was spotted parking his white Renault 5 in the square where the guard and regimental band were to form up prior to the regular Tuesday ceremony. It is believed that he parked there to hold a space for the car containing the bomb. Danny McCann and Mairead Farrell were then seen a little later, casually walking into Gibraltar from La Linea, the Spanish town adjoining the frontier with the Rock. They appeared relaxed.

At 2.50 p.m., all three met up in the square where the Renault was parked. It was at that time that the SAS brick, dressed in civvies, arrived on the scene. All were carrying Browning Hi-Power 9mm pistols. Soldiers A and B shadowed Savage, while Soldiers C and D shadowed McCann and Farrell. This posse of seven people mingled with the tourists and all walked towards the Almeda Gardens. At 3.25, all seven walked slowly back to the square, where Savage and McCann gave the vehicle a cursory glance before the three terrorists moved away, walking towards the frontier.

Immediately they had left the square, still walking slowly, an MI5 Explosive Ordnance Disposal Officer (EDO) went down to the square and examined the Renault from the outside. He advised those at Command Headquarters that it was possible that the car *could* contain a bomb. With that report, the SAS Commander took over control of Gibraltar from the civil police and the order to apprehend the three terrorists was passed by radio to the four SAS men.

The four SAS men walked some twenty yards behind their targets but not in a group; the three Provos walked together, seemingly chatting between themselves. They were nearing the Spanish frontier when Sean Savage suddenly turned and retraced his steps, walking back towards the square, while McCann and Farrell continued towards the frontier. At this point, the SAS brick changed targets: soldiers A and B turned and followed McCann and Mairead Farrell, while Soldiers C and D tracked Sean Savage back towards the square.

Those in Command Headquarters were now in a desperate dilemma. They realised they had only minutes to act before McCann and Farrell passed into Spanish territory and the SAS would then have had no right in law to arrest or shoot them. And they knew that their orders were to shoot and kill the three Provos.

At the inquiry that followed, Soldier A said in evidence that seconds after Savage had turned back from the frontier, a police car switched on its siren while trying to move through heavy traffic, causing McCann to turn his head and make eye contact with him. Soldier A maintained that McCann had realised two men were following him and alleged that he made a 'suspicious movement' with his right arm. Both Soldiers A and B said in evidence that they believed that arm movement might have meant he was reaching for a radio-controlled device to set off the bomb and they drew their pistols. Soldier A stated that he shouted a challenge before shooting McCann once in the back and then, seeing Farrell make a grab for her handbag, shooting her once in the back also. He then moved

199

forward and fired three more rounds into McCann while Soldier B fired two rounds at Farrell and five at McCann.

Sean Savage was some one hundred yards from his two accomplices when the firing began and he spun round to see what was happening. Soldier C allegedly shouted at him to stop. Later, Soldier C made a statement saying that he saw Savage reach for his pocket and, fearing he was about to activate a radio-controlled device, he drew his pistol and fired six shots at Savage while Soldier D fired nine: fifteen bullets in all. The entire action was over in four seconds.

At no time did the four SAS soldiers attempt to arrest the three IRA suspects and at no time were the Gibraltar police asked to intervene, question or arrest them. No attempt whatsoever was made to intercept or arrest the three IRA activists while they were on Spanish soil and at no time did Britain request the Spanish authorities to question, apprehend or arrest them on suspicion that they were engaged in terrorist activities. With the evidence the British already had on the ASU, and the fact that arms and explosives had been discovered in Malaga, it would have been quite a simple process to seek their arrest. The decision not to do so was, of course, a political decision taken at the very highest level in Downing Street. It must be noted that the Joint Intelligence Committee, frequently chaired by Prime Minister Thatcher, was kept informed of developments throughout Operation Flavius.

The shooting of Savage, McCann and Farrell at the hands of the SAS caused a furore in Ireland and the United States, mainly because no weapons were found on any of them and there was no bomb in the white Renault. Nor was there any sight of a radio-controlled device. However, the Provisional IRA did confirm that the three had been on a bombing mission and referred to them as martyrs, despite the fact that the 140 lb of Semtex was later found in the red Ford Fiesta in the car park at Edificio Marbeland in Marbella.

Intelligence sources have now revealed that before the inquest into the three killings was held, the four SAS men who were called to give evidence were all briefed by Ministry of Defence lawyers and mock inquests were held in which they were put under considerable pressure. They were briefed about exactly what they should say in evidence, briefed that their stories had to tally and repeatedly briefed about the reasons they opened fire. Nothing was left to chance. It seems that their evidence was sufficiently convincing because on Friday, 30 September 1988, an inquest jury gave its majority (nine to two) verdict: lawful killing.

However, those in the security services at the time have no doubt that Savage, McCann and Farrell were 'executed' that day and the decision to kill them had been taken in London by Prime Minister Thatcher and two other senior colleagues as a demonstration of the British Government's determination to carry the war to the IRA whenever and wherever possible. This single event also had the effect of persuading the IRA to tread carefully before organising terrorist atrocities outside Northern Ireland.

Chapter Nine

ACCIDENTS HAPPEN, MISTAKES OCCUR, FACTS IGNORED

'Mayday! Mayday! Mayday!' This dramatic call is used by pilots and seafarers the world over when disaster is imminent. Sometimes, however, the danger is explosive and immediate, giving no time whatsoever for an aircraft pilot to appeal for help to the nearest radio call centre.

This is precisely what happened at 6 p.m. on the evening of 2 June 1994, when Chinook HC2 ZD576 flew at a speed in excess of 100 mph into the Hill of Stone on the Mull of Kintyre, killing all 29 people on board. There was no time for any alert to be given by the pilot or co-pilot, and as a result there was an almost knee-jerk reaction among both army and intelligence officers, who were convinced that a bomb had been placed on the helicopter that day.

Due to the very nature of intelligence work, undercover operations, covert police surveillance and special forces tasks, there will always be genuine mistakes, accidents and plain errors that generate enormous interest, many theories and a myriad of suppositions, even falsehoods. Inevitably, politicians, journalists and those engaged in intelligence work will quite often rush to judgement, and in doing so will ignore plain, simple facts, supplanting them with theories that *could* fit.

It goes without saying that such theories nearly always point to dark forces at work. In the case of Northern Ireland during the past 30-odd years, more often than not these theories turned out to be remarkably accurate. Not only were the Provisional IRA and Loyalist paramilitaries constantly planning and carrying out bombings, shootings and killings but the forces of law and order ranged against them were also hard at work trying to contain them, sometimes by devious and illegal means.

As a result, many of those charged with the task of controlling the security situation on the ground were put under considerable political pressure from the Prime Minister down. Many incidents that occurred, if not carried out by the Provos or the Loyalists, were quite often the work of one or another of the various government agencies. But throughout those years, genuine accidents did still occur.

What made the Chinook crash particularly suspicious was that nearly all of those who died were military intelligence officers, many of them in senior and sensitive positions of authority, who were at the epicentre of intelligence gathering in Northern Ireland.

It seemed beyond belief that a Royal Air Force Chinook – one of the safest of helicopters – could have been flown accidentally into the side of a mountain when the two men flying the machine were highly experienced pilots with many years' service.

To this day, there are still those in Northern Ireland engaged in the political process who remain convinced that the Chinook crash was not an accident. They believe that the Chinook disaster, which hit at the very heart of the British Government's intelligence network in the province, was so fundamental and so damaging to the Government that an immediate and total cover-up was ordered by the Prime Minister. Indeed, had the crash been the result of a terrorist bomb, such a devastating breach of security would have been hugely embarrassing and would have all but destroyed the Government's claim to have the Northern Ireland security situation 'under control'.

The deaths of so many senior officers caused immediate and major problems for the intelligence services. And yet there was no drama and no chaos within the different agencies. Those men and women acting as deputies to the men killed in the crash were immediately promoted to the vacant positions and the job continued as though nothing had happened. Almost normal service resumed within a matter of a few days, though the experience and expertise of those killed was missed for some months. It was indeed a credit to the intelligence agencies that the effects of that crash were so minimal, when many expected it to take years to get over such a monumental and catastrophic event.

There had been nothing unusual about this flight for those in command – Flight Lieutenant Jonathan Tapper and Flight Lieutenant Richard Cook, both experienced special-forces pilots. Tapper, the non-handling pilot on this flight, had 2,081 flying hours with helicopters and had served in Oman. Cook, the so-called handling pilot, had 2,096 flying hours. Only a few weeks earlier, Cook had, in fact, landed the same Chinook on the H-shaped landing pad north of the Mull lighthouse, so he was fully acquainted with the terrain.

On this trip, Tapper and Cook were planning to fly across the Irish Sea to the Mull of Kintyre and then up the Great Glen towards Inverness. Their destination was Fort George, where the military intelligence agents were bound, principally, it was reported, for a weekend of work and debate in a quiet, secluded and peaceful setting. It was also accepted that the men would take time out to enjoy the odd round of golf at the nearby course. This weekend away from the Troubles of Northern Ireland had become an annual summer event for intelligence officers but senior officers who gave evidence at the subsequent inquest and later official inquiries all maintained that the main reason for the weekend in Scotland was to work.

However, there was one remarkable fact that has never before been revealed and which, at the time, caused much drama and dismay both in Belfast and London. At such gatherings of intelligence officers, the top-secret, classified material which the officers would be discussing and dissecting at the meeting is placed in a locked, secure steel box for transportation to and from the selected destination. As soon as the devastating news of the crash was relayed to London, the immediate response was to assert the urgent necessity of finding that steel box containing the top-secret material.

In the immediate aftermath, intelligence chiefs had to act on the belief that the crash was no accident but an act of terrorism on the part of the Provisional IRA. And, if the Provos had known that the Chinook would be taking off that day from Aldergrove RAF base outside Belfast, containing 25 intelligence agents on their way to an important meeting, it would be reasonable to assume that they would have suspected that also on board would be top-secret material they would dearly love to get their hands on.

Indeed, if the Provos had somehow managed to place a bomb on board, they might well have attempted to time the blast to occur when the chopper was over Scotland. It was well known that the Provos had a number of ardent supporters in Glasgow, as they have always done since the Troubles began. They could have been alerted to listen to the radio that day and have been prepared to race to the crash site and pick up the steel box as soon as they heard reports of a helicopter crash.

As soon as London was alerted to the crash, senior police officers in Glasgow were immediately tasked to get to the crash site as quickly as possible to secure the area. It was vital that no one without security clearance was permitted entry. Days and nights were spent by police, under the supervision of MI5 officers, not only sifting through the wreckage but also scouring the entire area surrounding the crash site in a determined, and increasingly desperate, bid to find the missing secret material. They were told the officers on board had been travelling to Scotland for an important meeting, as well as to enjoy a round of golf and a relaxing weekend, and therefore they were certain that a steel box containing classified material was bound to be on board.

What worried the intelligence services, of course, was that if the material fell into the hands of the Provisional IRA, all current and future plans of the intelligence agencies in Northern Ireland would have to be abandoned and new plans drawn up. Thousands of hours of careful work would have to be discarded. It cannot be known precisely what those intelligence papers would have included but it would be fair to suggest that they might well have revealed identities of agents and touts working undercover which could have put many lives in danger.

Even though such a meticulous search was carried out, no top-secret or classified material was ever found and no steel box was ever recovered. Though it has never been admitted by the authorities or by the Government, one is led to the inevitable conclusion that there was no classified material on board the Chinook because no work was in fact planned. The weekend at Fort George was simply a jolly, a few rounds of golf, a few pints of beer, a few good meals and a convivial get-together away from the Troubles. And, of course, all at the taxpayer's expense.

In spite of a thorough RAF investigation, a comprehensive report and an inquest which went on for three weeks, officially, the crash still remains a complete mystery. To those who favour conspiracy theories – and there are many in Northern Ireland who have good reason to believe in them – the reason the crash has remained a mystery is because the authorities have refused to permit the general public to know that the crash was caused by a bomb, presumably placed on board sometime before take-off from Aldergrove. Indeed, to many serious-minded people who have examined the facts of the case, though not the detail, a bomb is by far and away the most likely cause of the crash. It answers many of the questions which have been thrown up since the crash and which have never been satisfactorily answered by anyone.

In their report into the accident, the Government's investigation team reported the last words received from the chopper. At 5.55 p.m., Flight Lieutenant Tapper called the Scottish Military Air Traffic Control at Prestwick Airport: 'Scottish Military, good afternoon. This is Foxtrot Four Zero.' But there was no reply from Air Traffic Control. That is another mystery that has remained unsolved. It is extraordinary that no one in Scottish Military Air Traffic Control, who would most certainly have been expecting the chopper flight at that time, replied to Foxtrot Four Zero. And there has never been an explanation.

Some minutes later, in the picturesque village of Carnlough not far from the Mull of Kintyre, Ann Taylor saw Foxtrot Four Zero heading towards her. She would say later:

> I looked out and saw a twin-bladed helicopter flying past my house. This helicopter was low. It was flying in the glen and I could see the top of the glen over the top of it. The sound of it changed as it passed by my home and I thought it was going to land in a field. I moved to the landing and watched it. It flew down, slanting towards Carnlough harbour. It was flying low all the time. We have planes and helicopters flying around here quite a bit, but I have not seen any as low as this recently unless they were actually going to land. The weather was clear, but the Mull of Kintyre was obscured by mist.

At the Mull of Kintyre lighthouse, the keeper, David Murchie, was preparing to go off duty. He would tell the inquiry:

> At approximately 1755 hours on 2 June 1994, I was sitting in my living room with my wife Margaret when I heard the

sound of an approaching Chinook helicopter. I remarked that if he was going to land, he would have problems, as the fog was so dense. At that point I got up and made my way round to the seaward side of the engine-room building where I could hear the helicopter approaching from the south-west. I would estimate the visibility at this stage to be 15 to 20 metres at the most. The helicopter now sounded very close and did not seem to be terribly high. The noise appeared to pass to the east of the lighthouse. It became apparent that it was not going to land because there were no noise changes similar to other helicopters that I have heard land before.

Anthony Gresswell and his girlfriend Mary Green, who were holidaying together, had parked their car at the end of the public road on a steep hill above the lighthouse and walked down the hill towards the lighthouse to take some video footage. Just before six o'clock, they began walking back up the hill.

Anthony Gresswell told the inquiry:

> As we set off at the foot of the hill, we heard the sound of a helicopter approaching from the left of the lighthouse. We were facing the lighthouse. We could not see the helicopter at all, but the sound was getting louder and louder. We thought it was coming in to land at the helicopter pad, which was approximately 50 yards above us on the hill.

Mary Green said:

> It appeared to be flying very low – so much so that I thought it was going to land on the lighthouse heli-pad. I made my way to the heli-pad and shouted to Tony to get the video ready to record the helicopter landing. The helicopter

was very near and I thought it was directly overhead. The engine sounded perfectly normal and I did not have any indication that the helicopter was in distress.

The last person to see the Chinook was Shirley Crabtree, who was visiting the Mull of Kintyre with her husband Alan. She told the inquiry:

The weather was really bad. We couldn't see the hills on either side of us because of the thick mist. The mist was swirling around because the wind was quite strong. As we were walking towards our car, I heard a helicopter. It seemed to be flying from my right, from the sea, over the tops of our heads. It seemed very low and I thought it strange. I was surprised that they were flying in that weather. I don't know how they saw anything at all. As it passed over, I looked up and I am sure I saw the rotor blade whirling in the mist and I thought I saw a white light that wasn't flashing. I only saw it for a split second, but I remember saying to Alan that it seemed only the height of a house above us. It flew off to our left.

Another witness, Russell Ellacott, who was on a touring holiday with a friend, told the inquiry:

I was walking along when I felt something like a pressure all around me. On reflection it felt like the down-draught from a helicopter. I then heard a propeller turning around for about four or five seconds and then I heard an explosion. I immediately saw an orange glow and became aware of dense, thick smoke.

Lighthousekeeper David Murchie told the inquiry:

I had become concerned about the aircraft that had just passed overhead. I made my way to the north-west of the building and heard a loud thud immediately followed by a whooshing and whistling sound that I thought to be the rotor blades striking the ground.

His wife Margaret said:

> After hearing the helicopter pass over, the next sound I heard was a dull thud then a cracking sound followed by a 'swish' noise. The noise wasn't particularly loud. Within a few seconds I saw a fireball on the hillside to the left of where I'd heard the sound of the crash. Then everything went quiet. All this took place within about two minutes of first hearing the helicopter.

Anthony Gresswell told the inquiry that, as he was about to start videoing the helicopter landing:

> I heard a crumpling sound followed by a splintering sound and then silence. I guessed immediately what had happened. I turned round some seconds later and saw a ball of fire rolling down the hillside about 500 yards away.

Russell Ellacott also heard the helicopter crash. He said:

> I then saw things shooting into the air. It was like a fireworks display. Visibility at this time was about ten feet maximum. Strangely, despite feeling pressure around me and hearing an explosion, I did not see or hear the helicopter. With the density of the mist and smoke, I don't think I could have been more than 100 yards from the crash.

In fact, HC2 ZD576 had crashed just below the ridge of the mountain. At the moment of impact the fuselage began to disintegrate as the helicopter struck the mountain ridge slightly forward of the rear cargo ramp. This sent the Chinook into the air again as the floor of the cargo bay was ripped off and the chopper continued to disintegrate. For some four seconds, it was airborne before striking the mountainside a second and final time. As the helicopter broke into two main sections, it made a violent manoeuvre, its massive rotor blades chopping through its fragmented framework causing terrible injuries to the men inside. Finally it came to rest some 300 metres from the point of the initial impact, with the bodies of the dead men strewn over the whole area.

Russell Ellacott ran over to investigate with his friend Tony Bracher and later told the inquiry:

> The wind was very strong and was blowing across the face of the hill. We climbed up the hill to get above the mist. We could hardly breathe because of the smoke. When I looked down, I saw debris spread over a distance and a particularly big bit of metal that looked like the nose of a helicopter.
>
> I more or less walked on a man lying on his back on the hillside. He had a gaping wound on the right side of his head, but it didn't appear to be bleeding. His legs were disjointed and were lying at a strange angle. His eyes were open and his mouth was wide open. He had on a bright orange survival suit and was not burned. After this, I saw another body about 20 feet downhill, and he was also wearing an orange survival suit. Again he wasn't burned. In the immediate vicinity I counted another five or six bodies in what appeared to be heaps, all wearing orange-coloured survival clothing.
>
> Suddenly, something went off, sort of exploded and shot into the air from a bit of wreckage. I was terrified. I realised we couldn't do anything for the people in the helicopter. I

was frightened there might be other explosions. As we walked away I saw a vast amount of documents flying about in the wind. Many of them were heading out towards the sea.

These documents were in fact the flying instructions and newspapers. The steel crash-proof box containing the secret documents was never found.

One hour after the crash, the coastguard, the fire service, ambulances, police and doctors began to arrive at the scene, soon to be followed by RAF crash investigation teams, aviation experts, Ministry of Defence officials, Chinook helicopter investigators and members of the Inquiry Board team. Of course, no survivors were discovered and, importantly, no classified documents.

The cockpit, the forward rotary hub and the front end of the cargo bay were found on the ridge some 400 metres from the impact site. Near them lay the body of Flight Lieutenant Tapper and not far off was Load Master Malcolm Forbes. Eleven bodies were found thirty metres down the hillside towards the sea. Three other smaller sections were found scattered in a radius of some sixty metres from the cockpit wreckage.

For the first two weeks, the crash site was put off-limits to the general public and the army provided a 24-hour armed guard across the entire area. Later, the army was withdrawn and a police guard took over. For three months, the site was declared out of bounds in case further searches needed to be made for whatever reason.

Chinooks had crashed before. The most devastating accident occurred some eight years before in November 1986, when 40 oil workers plus the flight crew died after their Chinook plunged 500 feet into the North Sea. On that occasion it was established that faulty gearboxes were the probable cause of the accident. Further RAF Chinook accidents occurred in February 1987, May 1988 and two in 1989, but no one was killed in these crashes. Despite these incidents, among chopper pilots, and statistically, the Chinooks are regarded as one of the safest helicopters.

The only recommendation the Boards of Inquiry made for all these accidents was the need to fit all Chinook helicopters with accident data recorders 'at the earliest opportunity'. And yet, the helicopter that crashed off the Mull of Kintyre, killing all 29 on board, had *not* been equipped with a cockpit voice recorder, and this was some eight years after the first crash in the North Sea that had killed 45 men. The reason: fitting a voice recorder was considered a security risk for helicopters engaged in special services operations in case it should fall into enemy hands. The Ministry of Defence deliberately took the decision to ignore the recommendations, giving the excuse that 'voice recorders do not prevent accidents'.

After their investigations, the Board of Inquiry into the Mull of Kintyre crash 'considered it possible that the crew of the helicopter may have *misappreciated* [author's emphasis] the gradient of climb achievable at their high airspeed of 150 knots'. In other words, they were stating that they believed the crash was the result of pilot error.

However, for some reason that has never been explained, the Board of Inquiry made the decision to ignore problems that had occurred both on the day of the accident and the day before. A different crew flying HC2 ZD576 the previous day had complained of 'a lagging No. 1 Engine PTIT gauge'. This problem was allegedly cleared during diagnosis when the No. 1 and No. 2 gauges were interchanged by the groundcrew. But this same problem occurred earlier on the day of the accident when Tapper's crew checked the aircraft prior to take off for the Mull of Kintyre. Surprisingly, the Board of Inquiry decided that 'it was not a factor in the accident'.

There had also been other problems. Chinook HC2 ZD576 had a history of unforeseen malfunctions, mainly associated with the engine control system, including 'undemanded engine shutdown, engine run-up, spurious engine failure captions and misleading and confusing cockpit indications'. However, because the Board found no evidence of any such malfunctions during the fatal flight, they chose to ignore that Chinook's history of malfunctions.

Yet more recent malfunctions were revealed with HC2 ZD576. On 3 May 1994 – just one month before the tragedy – the senior officer from 230 Squadron reported the GPS superTANS system had failed to operate. Two days later, on 5 May, the GPS receiver and aerial had to be replaced and on 9 May the receiver had to be replaced a second time.

Rather importantly, two replacement engines had to be installed within two weeks of each other and yet, on 31 May, exactly three days before its last flight, the Chinook had arrived in Northern Ireland for operational use and passed as 'apparently serviceable'.

The Board did add a rider, saying:

> Nevertheless, an unforeseen technical malfunction of the type being experienced on the Chinook HC2, which would not necessarily have left any physical evidence, remained a possibility and could not be discounted . . . given the large number of unexplained technical occurrences on the Chinook HC2 since its introduction, the Board considered it possible that a technical malfunction or indication could have provided a distraction to the crew.

In other words, even the Board accepted that there was a possibility that the crew were dealing with a false emergency at a critical time, perhaps as the chopper approached the Mull, a distraction which may have lasted long enough to prove fatal.

However, the body blow which stunned the relatives of pilots Tapper and Cook came when three senior RAF officers took it upon themselves to blame both men for the crash, adding stinging statements in which one officer concluded that 'the actions of the two pilots were the direct cause of this crash. I also conclude that this amounted to gross negligence.'

Understandably, the families of the two pilots were distressed by the Board's findings but they were angered and some enraged by the harsh criticism of the three RAF officers who had laid the blame squarely on the shoulders of the two pilots. Two of those RAF officers were Air Marshals.

Many of the relatives of those who died in the tragedy were angered by the tactics of the Ministry of Defence, whose lawyers attempted to destroy the argument that the crash could have been caused by malfunctioning equipment and not by pilot error. When a witness, an RAF officer, suggested that a 'control jam' could have occurred, a Ministry of Defence lawyer disagreed, dismissing the idea with an outrageous remark: 'The chance that his version of events was correct was millions to one against.' Despite this put-down attempt, the witness continued to insist, time and again, that Tapper was much too good a pilot to have made errors that would have led to the tragedy.

But this would not be the end of the affair.

A House of Lords investigation into the crash found in 2002 that 'the RAF should not have blamed the pilots'. Indeed, the all-party committee of five peers went further, stating that the RAF Board of Inquiry was wrong to brand the pilots negligent.

The peers stressed that an investigating board and two station commanders 'made no findings of negligence'. They concluded that how the aircraft flew into the Mull, 'we shall never know'.

And yet the Ministry of Defence stuck to their guns, stating:

> The professional judgement of the reviewing officers, endorsed by the department, was and still is that the standard of proof was sufficient. The Lords report does not have judicial status and will have no direct effect on the validity of the original finding of negligence.

The Lords report was an undoubted victory for the families of the Chinook pilots who had battled for months to clear their names. Liberal Democrat foreign affairs spokesman Menzies Campbell called on the Government to quash the official finding of negligence:

> An injustice has been done. It must now be put right. The duty of the Government is now clear. They must accept the conclusions of the report, re-open the inquiry and quash the findings of negligence. Anything else would be totally unacceptable.

There are many with the Royal Air Force, as well as among the families of those who died in the crash, who believe that the reason the Ministry of Defence stuck so rigidly to the 'negligence' finding was the little matter of compensation. If the original Board of Inquiry had reported that the Chinook crash was, more than likely, down to equipment malfunctions and *not* pilot error, the amount of compensation paid to victims would have been far, far higher than that eventually handed out. And it is possible that a legal action might have been successful against not only the Ministry of Defence but also Boeing, the US aircraft makers, in a compensation claim.

As it was, of course, some compensation was paid to the families. The families of both Tapper and Cook were awarded compensation but only granted 50 per cent of what they were entitled to, the Ministry of Defence claiming that the findings of negligence, though not proven, meant that 50 per cent was a 'fair' adjudication of their responsibility for the crash.

However, despite the fact that the Mull of Kintyre Action Group continued their fight to clear the names of the two pilots, they were unsuccessful and the crash has forever remained an enigma. But the desperate fear, the immediate knee-jerk reaction to the crash, that the Provisional IRA had managed to place a bomb on the helicopter, has faded with time, primarily because no trace of a bomb was discovered in the wreckage. The explosion noises heard by witnesses were made by the helicopter smashing into the mountain and the explosion of the fuel tanks. And both coincided with the moment of impact. To all intents and purposes, those simple facts ruled out the possibility of a bomb.

Throughout the years of war that gripped the Province there have, of course, been many other occasions when the facts seemed to point towards some kind of cover-up by the authorities in an attempt to avoid blame being correctly, and perhaps uncomfortably, apportioned. In some instances, it has been alleged that this may have been an attempt to hide collusion between the authorities and those involved in killings. In some instances, such suspicions have been proved correct, as the intelligence agencies and the security forces fought an undercover war against the Provos. But there are many other killings that seemed at first to bear the hallmarks of collusion by the security services and which proved to be accidents.

Perhaps one of the most extraordinary involved a road accident between a tractor and a car driven by a well-known Provo activist, Brian 'Dipper' Dempsey, who had once owned a Belfast taxi firm. In the spring of 1987, Dempsey was driving at speed along a deserted country lane some 20 miles from Belfast when the tractor, hidden from view behind a screen of trees, suddenly appeared out of a farm gateway and drove straight into the path of his car.

In the vehicle with Dempsey were two men alleged to be high-profile Provo officers. The two men were reported to have been on their way to interrogate a suspected tout who they understood had been feeding information to the security services.

In a desperate attempt to avoid the lumbering tractor, Dempsey swerved, but the tractor still hit the car broadside. The three occupants were thrown around inside the car, which rolled over and over before ending up in the ditch by the side of the road.

Dempsey was killed outright and one of the other men was knocked unconscious and seriously injured. The third man panicked and simply ran away from the scene as fast as he could, fearful of being recognised as a PIRA activist and arrested if he stayed and waited for the RUC to arrive. He believed that both his comrades were dead so there was no point in waiting around. The shocked tractor driver was amazed to see that the third man was running from the scene, leaving his two friends dying at the roadside. The ambulancemen called to the scene pronounced Dempsey dead but his companion was taken to hospital with serious injuries.

The two survivors were convinced that the accident had been set up and carried out by members of the security forces. In the Republican pubs and clubs around Belfast the word was put about that the tractor driver was an MI5 agent who had been ordered to simply drive the tractor into the car in a bid to kill the three men. It was all untrue. The tractor driver was a farmer and had simply been driving out of the gateway to the field at the precise moment the Provo car was thundering down the road. He hadn't even seen the car until a split second before the crash.

Brian Dempsey was given a full PIRA funeral, with the coffin bearers wearing black masks and black armbands, and there was the traditional rifle salute at the graveside. One of the reasons why the Provos were so certain this had been a botched murder plot organised by MI5 was the fact that their notorious interrogator Steak Knife had told them that Dempsey had spoken to him about an MI5 agent who had tried to recruit him.

Steak Knife was simply quoting Dempsey, but the story gained credence when a mysterious wreath of flowers arrived at the graveside with a card reading 'MI5'. The wreath enraged the Provisional leadership and Dempsey's family, and also convinced them that MI5 had planned the murder of the three men. There was, however, little they could do to prove their suspicions.

But it was not the end of the affair. The Belfast PIRA Brigade questioned each and every one of the drivers at Dempsey's company, convinced that one of them must have been working as a tout for one of the intelligence or security agencies. For months afterwards, there was a fear that one of the drivers must have been a tout and, of course, the PIRA had convinced themselves, with a little help from Steak Knife, that the crash had been carried out in a bid to kill three of their men.

One of the most bizarre killings of the last 30 years occurred in May 1981, when two Provo gunmen were shot dead and a third seriously injured during a shoot-out in the Creggan area of Derry. Several different versions of the shooting were circulated at the time but this is the correct one.

A lone soldier, a member of the 14th Int., was driving a brown-coloured Opel Ascona car through Derry at about 12.30 p.m. when he saw a Ford Escort coming towards him with four men inside. As he passed by, the driver of the Escort raised his forefinger to the Opel driver, a sign of recognition often used by Provo activists in Derry, and he was surprised there was no return sign of recognition from the Opel driver.

It seemed the four men, all members of an IRA active service unit, were hell-bent on causing trouble that morning, because they had hijacked the Ford Escort from the Creggan area, locking the driver in a coalshed, where he remained for some 90 minutes.

Suspicious as to whom the Opel driver might be, the Escort driver spun the car round and gave chase. When the Ford Escort caught up with the Opel, the driver pulled in front of the car, forcing the Opel to stop. At the same time, shots were fired by two of the Escort passengers using Armalite rifles, one shot breaking the driver's window while other shots hit the driver's door. All four men in the Escort were wearing balaclavas. When the cars came to a halt, two gunmen jumped from the Escort and ran towards the Opel driver.

Fearing he was about to be killed, the Opel driver took out his

9mm Browning automatic and fired two shots as the first gunman ran towards his vehicle, hitting the gunman in the chest. As the man fell dying across the bonnet of the Opel car, his Armalite went off accidentally and six rounds pierced the bonnet of the Opel, two rounds imbedding themselves in the engine block.

The soldier then turned to face the other gunman, who was running towards his car from the rear. He fired two rounds from his Browning automatic, hitting the gunman in the throat. When the third gunman brought up his Armalite to shoot the soldier, he was simply too slow and the soldier fired off two more rounds, hitting him in the chest and abdomen. This man survived the shooting.

Fearing that the fourth gunman might also attack him, the soldier was desperate to escape and so he tried to dislodge the dead gunman's body, which was lying across the bonnet, by firing some six rounds into his body. He failed to dislodge the body but, fearing that he too might be shot, the fourth gunman fled the scene.

The two men who died were George Patrick McBrearty, a 23-year-old shop assistant from the Creggan, and Charles Paul Maguire, 21, also from the Creggan.

After these killings, the Derry Brigade of the IRA issued a statement claiming that the four Provo gunmen had chased the Opel car because they had recognised the driver as a known SAS undercover agent. The IRA statement read:

> They pursued and opened fire on the car. Almost immediately, two other cars, one a red Chrysler, the other a yellow Porsche with three SAS men, arrived at the scene and opened fire on the active service unit. The two volunteers who had stepped from the vehicle were hit before the SAS sped off. Local people came to the assistance of the ASU and got them away.

The killing of McBrearty and Maguire has always been disputed by the Derry Brigade but there has never been any evidence put forward that either a red Chrysler or a yellow Porsche were at the scene or that anyone else was involved in the shooting save for the four IRA gunmen and the 14 Company soldier.

There have, of course, been countless other accidents which have resulted in the deaths of many people during the long years of the Troubles, and there are always some people who maintain that no one has been killed accidentally. The odds must, however, be that some did indeed die that way.

AFTERWORD

Even when the sectarian war in Northern Ireland was at its height, those people involved in the conflict had as much to fear from Britain's secret intelligence agencies and security services as from those on the other side of the religious divide.

One of the more sinister aspects of the activities of the intelligence services operating in Northern Ireland throughout the Troubles was their use of touts and killers, both Loyalist and Provisional IRA, to carry out their dirty work in a deliberate attempt to blur the link between the intelligence services and the men who carried out the killings.

The unholy alliance between the three intelligence services – MI5, the RUC Special Branch and the Force Research Unit – and the killers on both sides of the sectarian divide was one of the more repugnant facts of life that began in the early 1970s and continued even after the turn of the century.

In this book, as in the revelations contained in *Ten-Thirty-Three* – which dealt with British Military Intelligence and their use of Loyalist gunmen to target and kill Republicans and members of the

Provisional IRA – I have sought to show how MI5 and the RUC Special Branch worked together and used Loyalist and Provo gunmen to commit murders on their behalf.

The team of detectives working with Sir John Stevens are still investigating various sectarian murders as well as possible collusion between the intelligence services and the perpetrators of some of those killings. While researching this book, I have been fortunate in receiving detailed information from members of the three intelligence agencies concerning the killings I have outlined here.

In the spring of 2004, as a result of Sir John Stevens' high-profile investigations into various killings and possible collusion between the intelligence services and Northern Ireland's paramilitary organisations, he sent files to the Director of Public Prosecutions on about 20 former members of the army and police regarding their alleged roles in Patrick Finucane's murder.

In April 2004, the Government announced the setting up of public inquiries into three controversial murders that occurred during the 30 years of the Troubles. However, the Government did not announce a public inquiry into Mr Finucane's murder because Kenneth Barrett, a former member of the UDA who admitted in a television programme that he shot Patrick Finucane, is awaiting trial. However, it is expected that a further inquiry into Mr Finucane's death will be ordered after Barrett's trial.

As an author I can only urge members of all those inquiry teams not to automatically accept the word of the intelligence agencies when listening to their evidence, simply because they have much to conceal and much to lose. And because they, too, have blood on their hands.

Nick Davies
2004